Evidence-based Practice in Social Work

Thinking Through Social Work

Evidence-based Practice in Social Work	ISBN 978 1 84445 611 6
Social Work, Social Policy and Older People	ISBN 978 1 84445 349 8

Transforming Social Work Practice

Applied Psychology for Social Work (second edition)	ISBN 978 1 84445 356 6
Communication and Interpersonal Skills in Social Work	ISBN 978 1 84445 610 9
Effective Practice Learning in Social Work	ISBN 978 1 84445 253 8
Effective Writing Skills for Social Work Students	ISBN 978 0 85725 417 7
Equality and Diversity in Social Work Practice	ISBN 978 1 84445 593 5
Groupwork Practice in Social Work (second edition)	ISBN 978 0 85725 502 0
Need, Risk and Protection in Social Work Practice	ISBN 978 1 84445 252 1
Personalisation in Social Work	ISBN 978 1 84445 732 8
Reflective Practice in Social Work (second edition)	ISBN 978 1 84445 364 1
Safeguarding Adults in Social Work (second edition)	ISBN 978 0 85725 401 6
Sensory Awareness and Social Work	ISBN 978 1 84445 293 4
Social Policy and Social Work	ISBN 978 1 84445 301 6
Social Work and Dementia	ISBN 978 0 85725 621 8
Social Work and Human Development (third edition)	ISBN 978 1 84445 380 1
Social Work and Mental Health (fourth edition)	ISBN 978 0 85725 493 1
Social Work in a Digital Society	ISBN 978 0 85725 677 5
Social Work Practice: Assessment, Planning, Intervention and Review (third edition)	ISBN 978 1 84445 831 8
Studying for your Social Work Degree (second edition)	ISBN 978 0 85725 381 1
Understanding and Using Theory in Social Work (second edition)	ISBN 978 0 85725 497 9
Using Counselling Skills in Social Work	ISBN 978 0 85725 629 4
Using the Law in Social Work (fifth edition)	ISBN 978 0 85725 405 4
Values and Ethics in Social Work (second edition)	ISBN 978 1 84445 370 2
What is Social Work? Context and Perspectives (third edition)	ISBN 978 1 84445 248 4
Working with Aggression and Resistance in Social Work	ISBN 978 0 85725 429 0
Youth Justice and Social Work (second edition)	ISBN 978 0 85725 319 4

To order, please contact our distributor: BEBC Distribution, Albion Close, Parkstone, Poole, BH12 3LL. Telephone: 0845 230 9000, email: learningmatters@bebc.co.uk. You can also find more information on each of these titles and our other learning resources at www.learningmatters.co.uk

Evidence-based Practice in Social Work

IAN MATHEWS

and

KARIN CRAWFORD

First published in 2011 by Learning Matters Ltd

British Library Cataloguing in Publication Data
A CIP record for this book is available from the British Library

ISBN: 978 1 84445 611 6

This book is also available in the following ebook formats:

Adobe ebook ISBN: 978 1 84445 773 1
EPUB ebook ISBN: 978 1 84445 772 4
Kindle ISBN: 978 0 85725 027 8

Cover design by Toucan Design
Text design by Topics – The Creative Partnership
Project Management by Deer Park Productions
Typeset by Pantek Arts Ltd
Printed and bound in Great Britain by Bell & Bain Ltd, Glasgow

Learning Matters Ltd
20 Cathedral Yard
Exeter EX1 1HB
Tel: 01392 215560
info@learningmatters.co.uk
www.learningmatters.co.uk

Contents

Acknowledgements

We owe a debt of thanks to many people for their assistance in the production of this book. We would like to especially thank Kate Lodge and Luke Block at Learning Matters for their patient support over the many months that this book has taken to appear. We would also like to thank our colleagues and professional tea drinkers Diane and Emily for their companionship.

Ian Mathews dedicates this book to his parents Fred and Mary Mathews, with much love and gratitude.

Introduction

Over recent decades there has been considerable debate regarding the basis and legitimacy of social work practice. A cursory glance at the reports into the deaths of children such as Victoria Climbié or Peter Connelly (Laming 2003, 2009) confirms that the organisation, management and practice of social work is often open to governmental and public critique. Partly in response to these criticisms and other systemic issues profound changes are planned to the way that social work is organised and delivered over the next few years. For example, the General Social Care Council, the professional body of social work, is to be abolished, social work training is to be reconfigured, and the creation of a College of Social Work has been proposed. This ongoing critique also includes discussion regarding the validity and strength of the evidence base that underpins practice. After all, if the foundations of practice are uncertain or unable to withstand scrutiny, it is unlikely that the practice based on this knowledge will be successful. This book then is about how social work produces, uses, and evaluates the evidence and knowledge that underpins and informs professional practice.

Who is this book for?

The book is primarily intended for students who are completing a qualifying degree programme in social work, or for qualified practitioners who are undertaking PQ (Post-Qualifying) study. Additionally, we hope that other students or workers from health and social care backgrounds will also find the book useful as it addresses a number of themes which are common to a range of professional disciplines. The examples and exercises we use in this book are generic in nature and reflect issues across a range of practice areas.

We are aware that sometimes the complex nature of the questions we raise in the book means that some familiarity with professional practice may be necessary. Nonetheless, even those of you with minimal practice experience will be able to engage with the issues as they address many core components of social work. As so often, a willingness to undertake wider reading will also enhance your understanding. A range of helpful materials are identified at the conclusion of each chapter. The book is interactive in style and we would encourage you to engage with the critical thinking exercises in each chapter as they will broaden your understanding of the debates we raise and increase your ability to analyse complex ideas.

The Quality Assurance Agency Subject Benchmarks for Social Work

Throughout this book explicit links are made to the Subject Benchmarks for Social Work developed by The Quality Assurance Agency (QAA). The intention is to help those students who are studying for a social work degree to make links between the book and their academic/professional development.

What are 'Subject benchmark statements?'

According to the Quality Assurance Agency website (**www.qaa.ac.uk**) 'Subject benchmark statements set out expectations about standards of degrees in a range of subject areas. They describe what gives a discipline its coherence and identity, and define what can be expected of a graduate in terms of the abilities and skills needed to develop understanding or competence in the subject.'

The benchmarks are not intended to be seen as a set national curriculum but they do establish expectations about the knowledge, skills, understanding, and competence that social work students will be expected to attain by the end of their degree.

Throughout this book we will suggest at the commencement of each chapter which Subject Benchmarks statements for social work are especially helpful for you to consider as you read the chapter. We have provided a selection of appropriate benchmark statements below to illustrate the areas that you will be asked to reflect upon.

5.1 During their degree studies in social work, honours graduates should acquire, critically evaluate, apply and integrate knowledge and understanding in the following five core areas of study.

5.1.1 Social work services, service users and carers, which include:

the social processes (associated with, for example, poverty, migration, unemployment, poor health, disablement, lack of education and other sources of disadvantage) that lead to marginalisation, isolation and exclusion, and their impact on the demand for social work services;
explanations of the links between definitional processes contributing to social differences (for example, social class, gender, ethnic differences, age, sexuality and religious belief) to the problems of inequality and differential need faced by service users;
the nature of social work services in a diverse society with particular reference to concepts such as prejudice, interpersonal, institutional and structural discrimination, empowerment and anti-discriminatory practices;
the nature and validity of different definitions of, and explanations for, the characteristics and circumstances of service users and the services required by them, drawing on knowledge from research, practice experience, and from service users and carers;

the focus on outcomes, such as promoting the well-being of young people and their families, and promoting dignity, choice and independence for adults receiving services;
the relationship between agency policies, legal requirements and professional boundaries in shaping the nature of services provided in interdisciplinary contexts and the issues associated with working across professional boundaries and within different disciplinary groups.

5.1.2 The service delivery context, which includes:

the location of contemporary social work within historical, comparative and global perspectives, including European and international contexts;
the changing demography and cultures of communities in which social workers will be practising;
the complex relationships between public, social and political philosophies, policies and priorities and the organisation and practice of social work, including the contested nature of these;
the issues and trends in modern public and social policy and their relationship to contemporary practice and service delivery in social work;
the significance of legislative and legal frameworks and service delivery standards including the nature of legal authority, the application of legislation in practice, statutory accountability and tensions between statute, policy and practice;
the current range and appropriateness of statutory, voluntary and private agencies providing community-based, day-care, residential and other services and the organisational systems inherent within these;
the significance of interrelationships with other related services, including housing, health, income maintenance and criminal justice, where not an integral social service;
the contribution of different approaches to management, leadership and quality in public and independent human services;
the development of personalised services, individual budgets and direct payments;
the implications of modern information and communications technology (ICT) for both the provision and receipt of services.

5.1.3 Values and ethics, which include:

the nature, historical evolution and application of social work values;
the moral concepts of rights, responsibility, freedom, authority and power inherent in the practice of social workers as moral and statutory agents;
the complex relationships between justice, care and control in social welfare and the practical and ethical implications of these, including roles as statutory agents and in upholding the law in respect of discrimination;
aspects of philosophical ethics relevant to the understanding and resolution of value dilemmas and conflicts in both interpersonal and professional contexts;
the conceptual links between codes defining ethical practice, the regulation of professional conduct and the management of potential conflicts generated by the codes held by different professional groups.

5.1.4 Social work theory, which includes:

research-based concepts and critical explanations from social work theory and other disciplines that contribute to the knowledge base of social work, including their distinctive epistemological status and application to practice;
the relevance of sociological perspectives to understanding societal and structural influences on human behaviour at individual, group and community levels;
the relevance of psychological, physical and physiological perspectives to understanding personal and social development and functioning;
social science theories explaining group and organisational behaviour, adaptation and change;
models and methods of assessment, including factors underpinning the selection and testing of relevant information, the nature of professional judgement and the processes of risk assessment and decision-making;
approaches and methods of intervention in a range of settings, including factors guiding the choice and evaluation of these;
user-led perspectives;
knowledge and critical appraisal of relevant social research and evaluation methodologies, and the evidence base for social work.

5.1.5 The nature of social work practice, which includes:

the characteristics of practice in a range of community-based and organisational settings within statutory, voluntary and private sectors, and the factors influencing changes and developments in practice within these contexts;
the nature and characteristics of skills associated with effective practice, both direct and indirect, with a range of service users and in a variety of settings;
the processes that facilitate and support service user choice and independence;
the factors and processes that facilitate effective interdisciplinary, interprofessional and interagency collaboration and partnership;
the place of theoretical perspectives and evidence from international research in assessment and decision-making processes in social work practice;
the integration of theoretical perspectives and evidence from international research into the design and implementation of effective social work intervention, with a wide range of service users, carers and others;
the processes of reflection and evaluation, including familiarity with the range of approaches for evaluating service and welfare outcomes, and their significance for the development of practice and the practitioner.

QAA (2008)

The above benchmarks are taken from the QAA website (**www.qaa.ac.uk**) where further information can be found regarding how these benchmarks were devised and the wider role of the agency. To an extent, all of the chapters address all of the subject benchmarks as we analyse and critique the knowledge foundations of practice. This may seem a little ambitious but the specific purpose of this book is to assist you to develop an informed understanding of the breadth and complexity of professional practice.

Skills development

In addition to making links with the subject benchmark statements we will also be suggesting how this book can be used to develop a set of analytical skills which enhance professional practice. The skills we will be emphasising are:

skill 1	demonstrating understanding and application of theoretical ideas
skill 2	comparing and contrasting different viewpoints and experiences
skill 3	relating different views to underlying philosophies or ideologies
skill 4	evaluating different perspectives and ideas
skill 5	evaluating evidence
skill 6	synthesising arguments
skill 7	reflection
skill 8	reviewing, re-evaluating and reformulating your own views

This book assumes that you are generally familiar with the purpose of theory, what is distinctive about academic writing, and how to begin to engage in analysis and reflection. If you feel uncertain about these skills there are a range of books which will be of assistance. For undergraduate students on social work qualifying programmes there are books that cover basic study skills (Walker 2008) and critical learning skills (Jones 2009), while for PQ students there are books on critical thinking such as Brown and Rutter (2008).

Applying knowledge to practice: What is in this book?

While this book will introduce you to a number of wide-ranging debates we hope that you can see that a number of themes are interwoven throughout the chapters; for example, the interconnection between knowledge, evidence, values and skills. While the purpose of this book is to discuss and analyse knowledge and evidence, we consistently maintain that it is impossible to separate these component parts of good practice. Secondly, we argue that knowledge and evidence needs to be scrutinised to ensure that it is relevant and reliable. Another theme is the importance we place on understanding how knowledge that emanates from the views and perspectives of service users and carers provides an essential contribution to the research and knowledge that underpins and shapes ethical professional practice. Finally, a core question which runs throughout the book seeks to challenge our assumptions and understandings of knowledge: 'Is one form of knowledge better than any other form of knowledge?' Often we, both individually and as a society, view scientific knowledge generated by rigorous research methods as being the 'gold standard'. Is this true? Or in social work practice could we argue that other forms of knowledge such as 'practice wisdom' are of equal validity?

In order to prepare you for the journey we now provide a brief synopsis of each chapter.

Chapter 1 introduces you to a number of central themes which we return to throughout this book. For example, we start by inviting you to consider if and why social work requires knowledge and evidence to underpin the tasks that it does. This critical analysis represents an ideal opportunity to develop an understanding of theoretical ideas (skill 1).

We then move on to an even more challenging issue: the differences and commonalities between the key terms 'evidence' and 'knowledge'. This argument is a recurrent theme throughout the book and this chapter purely aims to provide the framework for a continuing debate. Sometimes these terms are taken as being indivisible. Our argument is that they are different and that both terms require critical interrogation if they are to be accepted as a basis for practice. Even at this early stage we hope that you can see that such a key debate enables you to use the following skills:

Skill 2 comparing and contrasting different viewpoints and experiences;

Skill 3 relating different views to underlying philosophies or ideologies;

Skill 4 evaluating different perspectives and ideas.

Without wishing to overemphasise the point you will see that many of the critical skills we encourage you to develop require you to compare and contrast competing views and theoretical positions. This book purposely incorporates a wide range of differing ideas which we hope will enable you to sharpen your analytical skills.

We then pose a question which is both philosophical and practical in nature. If social work is underpinned by evidence and knowledge, how reliable are these foundations? Is evidence and knowledge 'true' or does it need to be constantly reviewed and refined (skill 3)? The nature of truth is clearly contested and again we will be asking you to consider a range of positions.

Chapter 2 continues to analyse the foundations of social work practice and extends our debate to consider how knowledge is classified and categorised. Given the complexities of social work and the breadth of knowledge required to undertake the task, it is perhaps not surprising that typologies and systems of categorisation often appear to be unsatisfactory (skill 2). We spend some time exploring the way in which categories overlap and how they influence and interact with one another. For example, practitioner knowledge (also known as practice wisdom) is essentially knowledge generated through experience. Nonetheless, this type of knowledge is shaped by a range of other types of knowledge, such as policy and legislation, service user knowledge and the contribution of research (skills 4 and 6).

Chapter 3 begins to explore the practical application of knowledge in social work practice. A central plank of our argument is that knowledge, however it is viewed or defined, needs to serve a practical purpose otherwise there is a danger that it remains purely part of an abstract debate. We further argue that in order for knowledge to be 'fit for purpose' it needs to be questioned by the practitioner. In this chapter we briefly discuss two processes, reflective practice and supervision, which can assist the practitioner to analyse knowledge (skill 5). While these vehicles are clearly of importance they are merely examples of ways in which knowledge can be assessed and verified. Finally, in this chapter we raise some important considerations regarding the value base of social work and how we need to guard against an uncritical acceptance of knowledge without first questioning the basis of how that knowledge has been produced (skill 8). You will notice that a consistent theme throughout this book is the interrelationship between values and knowledge. Our argument is that it is neither wise nor possible to separate one from the other.

Chapter 4 continues to explore the underpinning evidence base of social work and raises a critical question: is it possible to define this knowledge base? For example, some commentators suggest that social work is such a fluid and increasingly specialist activity that there can be no agreement as to what constitutes 'core' knowledge (skills 3, 4 and 6). With this notion of evolution in mind, we move the debate forward by suggesting three factors which may stimulate change and creativity in the knowledge base of social work.

These are:

- the growing influence of service user knowledge;
- the demands placed on social work knowledge by interprofessional settings and cultures;
- an examination of lessons that can be learnt from inquiries and reports produced in response to high-profile failings in health and social care.

Chapter 5 analyses how the production of knowledge has moved away from traditional localities, notably formal research undertaken by university staff, and is now generated by a range of stakeholders with divergent perspectives and interests (skills 2, 3 and 8). In particular we consider three groups of potential researchers: service users and carers; practitioners; and students; and provide current examples to illustrate how these groups are influencing the production of knowledge. As always we endeavour to provide a balanced view and highlight some of the difficulties of engaging 'non-traditional' groups in research activity. This debate is especially topical and you may be able to reflect on opportunities you have to influence the production of knowledge (skills 7 and 8).

Chapter 6 commences by attempting to predict how some of the current influences on knowledge and evidence will evolve in the future. While this debate lacks certainty it provides a useful opportunity to discuss significant emerging drivers such as the Newly Qualified Social Worker Framework, the role of *The Social Work Reform Board* and the potential impact of the *Proposed Professional Capabilities Framework for Social Workers in England.* This chapter, like the rest of this book, encourages you to critique and reflect on your knowledge. For example, it raises questions about how social workers understand issues such as 'spirituality' and 'community', both of which feature in guidance documentation such as the *Proposed Professional Capabilities Framework for Social Workers in England* (skills 1, 2, 3, 4, 7 and 8). This chapter also discusses the influence of 'globalisation' and how social workers are now in a position to export what they consider to be knowledge to different parts of the world or into different sectors of the economy within the UK. This fluidity raises some concerns about the validity of social work training and how 'fit for purpose' it is in a highly mobile world.

Chapter 7 seeks to consolidate your learning by reviewing the key themes that are threaded throughout each preceding chapter. By way of a reminder these themes are listed below.

- The use and development of evidence and knowledge, alongside values, ethics and skills, forms the basis of effective social work professional practice.
- Evidence and knowledge for social work practice needs to be subjected to critical reflection, scrutiny and interrogation to ensure it is relevant, reliable, trustworthy and contextually appropriate.
- It is important to understand how knowledge that emanates from the views and perspectives of service users and carers provides an essential contribution to the research and knowledge that underpins and shapes ethical professional practice.

This concluding chapter is structured around a discussion of each of these themes and summarises the main issues that have emerged across this book, highlighting the connections between them. The chapter closes by re-examining the fundamental principles that underpin evidence-based practice in social work.

We hope that you enjoy this book and find it valuable. Given the breadth and fluidity of the subject area it is unlikely that this book will provide many cast-iron answers. But we hope that you find the debate stimulating and are encouraged to further explore the knowledge that underpins professional practice.

Part One

1 What underpins social work practice?

Karin Crawford

Achieving a Social Work Degree

Exercises in this chapter will focus on

- skill 1 demonstrating understanding and application of theoretical ideas
- skill 2 comparing and contrasting different viewpoints and experiences
- skill 3 relating different views to underlying philosophies or ideologies
- skill 4 evaluating different perspectives and ideas

Its content is particularly relevant to the following Social Work Subject Benchmarks.

4.7 the ability to acquire and apply the habits of critical reflection, self-evaluation and consultation, and make appropriate use of research in decision-making about practice and in the evaluation of outcomes

5.1.4 the ability to acquire and apply research-based concepts and critical explanations from social work theory and other disciplines that contribute to the knowledge base of social work, including their distinctive epistemological status and application to practice

5.1.5 the ability to acquire and apply processes of reflection and evaluation, including familiarity with the range of approaches for evaluating service and welfare outcomes, and their significance for the development of practice and the practitioner

Introduction

This chapter introduces you to a number of critical themes to which we will keep returning throughout the book. As you actively consider these themes you will be invited to undertake a range of skill development exercises which assist your thinking. For example, we start by inviting you to consider if and why professional social work requires knowledge and evidence to underpin the tasks that it does. This may seem a straightforward, almost commonsensical, debate but sometimes it is helpful to articulate the foundations of social work and explore why we undertake the task in the way that we do.

We hope that you will be able to see a sequence within this foundational chapter, as many of the arguments we raise recur in different guises throughout this book. Having invited you to consider the basis of social work we then move on to a challenging philosophical debate as we analyse the differences and commonalities between 'evidence' and 'knowledge'. At this stage in your reading you may reason that they mean the same thing and indeed they are often used in a casual way which does not reflect their inherent complexity. Our argument is that they are different and that both require critical interrogation if they are to be accepted as a basis for practice.

We then pose a number of associated questions which are critical to practice. If social work is underpinned by evidence and knowledge, how reliable are these foundations? Is evidence and knowledge 'true' or does it need to be constantly reviewed and reinterpreted in the light of new insights? How does our understanding of knowledge which is deemed central to good practice evolve over time? These questions may seem a little overwhelming but an essential skill that you will need to develop as a social worker is the ability to critically analyse arguments and complex information in order to become an effective practitioner (Keen et al. 2009). We hope that this book provides an excellent start to that process by giving you a succession of contentious ideas to dissect and debate.

Finally in this chapter, we discuss a number of ways of categorising knowledge. This provides a helpful summary of the critical analysis you will have done and also demonstrates that there are a number of valid ways of considering underpinning knowledge. The purpose of this first chapter is to introduce a range of recurring themes and to set the context for a critical debate of the foundations of social work. We hope you enjoy the challenge!

Evidence and knowledge: The basis of social work?

A widely accepted definition of social work provided by the International Federation of Social Workers (IFSW) suggests that

> “*The social work profession promotes social change, problem solving in human relationships and the empowerment and liberation of people to enhance well-being. Utilising theories of human behaviour and social systems, social work intervenes at the points where people interact with their environments. Principles of human rights and social justice are fundamental to social work.*”
>
> **IFSW** (2000)

While this definition is now a little dated and is open to challenge, it has been welcomed by many practitioners who appreciate the way it incorporates reference to social action, a theoretical basis and important value concepts such as rights and justice, all of which are integral to the way that social work operates.

The reference to theory, however, seems to have a minor role within the definition compared to the emphasis on the 'doing' of the task: problem solving, empowerment, liberation, intervenes, interact and so on. It could be suggested that this reflects the idea that social work is often viewed as being principally a practical activity based on little more than good personal skills. Margaret Thatcher, Conservative Prime Minister from 1979 to 1990, once allegedly claimed that social work was purely a matter of common sense which could best be undertaken by experienced mothers. Politicians, however, are not alone in entering the debate regarding the basis of effective social work. For example, **Nygren and Soydan** (1997: 218) suggest that

> *Social work is considered to be an activity that is not and cannot be based on book knowledge. Its success depends on personal talent, and it can be taught through learning by doing and by imitating experienced social workers.* ”

While the characteristics suggested by these authors – life experience, personal talent and common sense – are undoubtedly valuable assets to bring to social work, such quotations devalue the complex mix of skills, expertise and knowledge that underpins and informs the professional task.

To return to the IFSW (2000) definition we have to acknowledge that it is now some years old and does not fully reflect the intensity of the debate regarding the evidence base of social work that has occurred in more recent years. We would now like you to engage in that debate.

Why is underpinning evidence and knowledge important to social work practice?

Critical thinking exercise 1.1

Make a list of the reasons why you think that social work requires knowledge and evidence to underpin the practice it undertakes and the decisions that it makes.

We will be returning to this argument on a number of occasions, but as a starting point we want to highlight several important factors.

Firstly the general public expect professional workers to have a sound basis for their decisions and views and to be able to evidence them if necessary. On occasions our trust in some professional groups such as doctors or solicitors is implicit. The range of knowledge and expertise and the complexity of the information that they are required to know is so considerable that the general public tend to defer to their professional decision-making. Even so, there is a growing culture of challenging such professionals to justify and evidence the decisions that they make. This is equally the case in social work where decisions of profound and lasting importance need to be made.

Secondly, the practice of social work, and its place in the interprofessional environment, is enhanced if a worker is able to demonstrate to users and to colleagues in other agencies the rationale for action/inaction and some of the research and information which has guided their thinking. It is inappropriate to expect the public at large or other groups of professionals to have respect for social work if it comes across as ill-informed and little more than instinctive. An ability to analyse evidence and to reflect on the validity of this evidence is an important social work skill. Taylor (2010), in his discussion of decision-making within social work, suggests that a holistic approach focuses on a range of crucial questions.

In relation to decision making a consideration of role alerts us to seeing ourselves as one player within what is often a complex situation, but nonetheless a useful contributor with a particular range of knowledge and skills. Among professions, social workers tend to have a holistic perspective on situations. The factors that we take into account in order to make sense of a complex, changing mosaic of information may be described as framing the decision.

These factors include:

- law, regulations, policies, procedures;
- function of your organisation and services available;
- relevant functions and services of other organisations;
- values, standards, principles;
- knowledge, research, theory and skills.

Adapted from **Taylor** (2010: 62)

This quote is helpful as it begins to articulate and explore some of the threads of knowledge and evidence that social workers are required to use in order for their work to be seen as credible by the public and by other professionals. Social workers are also required to demonstrate that their decisions are based on robust evidence in more formal arenas. For example, social workers are increasingly required to argue their case in court settings, to formally established panels with executive powers, to inquiries and to committees of politicians and others with influence on service outcomes. The people who sit on such fora may have a varying understanding of social work practice and policy. They are usually interested in the specific evidence being presented to justify a course of action especially when that action requires the allocation of scarce resources or the removal from home of a person against their will. These important decision-making fora and service users are best served by well-informed social workers who can present a case which is underpinned by sound evidence.

There are also important moral/ethical reasons as to why social work should be an informed activity. People who use services have a right to know that the judgements made by social workers which profoundly affect them and their families are made on something more substantial than personal opinion or common sense. For example, it is unethical to work with an older person towards the provision of permanent care in a residential setting and presenting it as a positive choice if you have not considered research into the effects of institutionalisation and the risks involved in moving people from their homes late in life. It is immoral to intervene in people's lives without any clear idea as to the potential effects of the work being undertaken and without knowing if their situation is likely to be improved or be made worse as a result of your intervention.

Optional further study

You will find an interesting and accessible discussion of the moral and ethical reasons behind decision-making in mental health social work in Bogg (2010). Chapter 2 in particular offers an historical overview of the various ethical perspectives and the role of social work

Social workers not only have a moral duty to acquire a sufficient quantity and quality of knowledge to explain and justify their decision-making, they also have an obligation to keep their knowledge current and up to date. In practice, where workers have to balance many competing demands and pressures, this is sometimes not easy. Social workers, however, frequently expect service users to learn new skills, to absorb new information and to evidence their ability to change. If service users cannot adapt in this way, they risk having their children removed, being institutionalised or experiencing other unwanted outcomes. It would be unethical if those demanding and monitoring change and learning from service users were not able to similarly evidence the capacity for change and growth in their own professional practice.

Later in this book, in Chapter 7, we will be analysing the *Proposed Professional Capabilities Framework for Social Workers in England* which is currently being promoted by the *Social Work Reform Board*. The proposed framework will guide all aspects of social work training and will be used to make judgements about the capabilities of staff at all levels of responsibility. While it is not certain that this framework will be adopted it is a significant indicator of the way in which social work practice will be monitored in the future. Interestingly, the first capability is

> *Professionalism: Identify and behave as a professional social worker, committed to professional development.*
>
> *Social workers are members of an internationally recognised profession, a title protected in UK law. Social workers demonstrate professional commitment by taking responsibility for their conduct, practice and learning, with support through supervision. As representatives of the social work profession they safeguard its reputation and are accountable to the professional regulator.*
>
> **HM Government** (2010)
>
> As can be seen, the proposed framework explicitly confirms the need for social workers at all stages of their careers to commit themselves to ongoing professional development and learning.

Another reason why social workers need to underpin their practice with evidence and knowledge is that otherwise there is a risk that their work becomes solely based on intuition or 'practice wisdom'. We return to an analysis of practice wisdom on a number of occasions but for now we will simply define it as knowledge which is accumulated through the experience of undertaking professional practice. Sometimes there is a danger that this knowledge can be overly intuitive bordering on the commonsensical. A 'common sense approach' is not a valid professional approach as what may seem 'common sense' to one person may seem entirely inappropriate to another. Common sense is difficult to define but may be influenced by an array of factors, such as family upbringing, religion, education, social class, age, gender, culture, social norms and the policies and laws of the country in which the person has grown up and the one in which they now live. Social workers clearly need to have common sense but they are required to be critical thinkers and to apply knowledge to their practice. Doing whatever comes naturally may be damaging, especially if what comes naturally is prejudicial, ill-informed or plain wrong (D'Cruz and Jones 2004).

Finally, there is an increasing need for social work to demonstrate that it is a profession that fulfils an important and legitimate function. Social work has historically been poor at defining its purpose and contribution, particularly when compared with other allied professions such as nursing and medicine (Bogg 2008). Equally, the notion of social work being a profession does not fit well with some who are uneasy with the inherent connotations of power, control, prestige and 'professional imperialism' that often accompany the term (Horner 2009; Simpkin 1983). These arguments aside, an integral part of contemporary social work is the ability to know what you need to know in order to provide a good, professional service. There is, of course, considerable debate as to what this knowledge is, but poorly informed, ill-judged and unbalanced intervention has all too often tarnished the reputation of social work. For example, the inquiry into

Haringey Council's handling of the Victoria Climbié case noted that social workers and other professional staff misinterpreted Victoria's signs of distress, ignored indicators of sexual abuse and deemed that overchastisement could be legitimised as a 'cultural nuance'. (Laming 2003). A basic knowledge of child behaviour, child protection policy and the ability to look beyond the claims of her carers was sadly lacking.

Critical thinking exercise 1.2

Having begun to discuss why evidence and knowledge are important to social work practice we now want you to consider a different set of questions.

1. Can social work claim to have its own unique knowledge base? Or does it merely borrow from other professions and a range of academic disciplines?
2. If so, is this problematical?
3. Does this call into question the legitimacy of social work?

In relation to the first question some well-established professions such as law or medicine would have little difficulty in making a response as their evidence base is well defined and protected. We feel, however, that it is problematical to claim that social work has its own unique knowledge base. There are of course considerable elements of expertise, such as knowledge relating to legislation and policy, the application of theory, the use of research and so on, but few if any of these are uniquely the domain of social work. As we shall explore later, the knowledge base of social work is wide and draws on a multitude of sources. Rather than being a hindrance to practice it may be that this diversity gives social work an advantage as practitioners are not overly restricted in the knowledge that is available to them. As Trevithick (2005: 28) argues, 'this has produced a potentially rich and diverse knowledge base' for the profession. It does, however, sometimes lead the credibility of social work into question as most definitions of what constitutes a profession demand a rigorous body of knowledge which is specific to that occupation.

Evidence and knowledge: A crucial debate

You may have noticed that we have consistently used the terms 'evidence' and 'knowledge'. Some of you may feel that there is little difference between these concepts and that they can be used interchangeably. In some discussions this may be the case, but we now want to critically explore this argument and suggest that evidence and knowledge, while related, are separate components of the foundations that underpin professional social work.

Over recent years there has been a plethora of books and journal articles written about 'evidence-based practice'. Government reports and the work of the Social Care Institute for Excellence (SCIE) often promote the claim that the best social work intervention is based on 'evidence' (SCIE 2004b). The term evidence-based practice is not new and is not restricted to social work practice, having been a feature of other allied disciplines such as nursing, psychology and medicine for many years (Corby 2006). In itself this is interesting as there is an argument that these occupations are seeking to be seen as increasingly scientific in the way they work. Scientific research and the evidence it produces is often portrayed as being stronger and more reliable than any other form of enquiry. Consequently, those professions that can claim to have a scientific basis for their work tend to be better regarded by the public and be able to gain more power and control over the work they do.

CASE STUDY

The rise of psychiatry

In his well-regarded critique of the medicalisation of mental illness, Scull (1993) traces the rise to dominance of that branch of medicine we know as psychiatry. In the early decades of the nineteenth century, the limited amount of care available to mentally ill people was provided by the church or the local parish. It was ad hoc and poorly organised with mental illness often being viewed as the result of religious or spiritual issues or as a physical condition.

As the century progressed, however, the growth of rational enquiry and science led to a very different understanding of insanity – that it was a disease of the brain. The mentally ill consequently required a qualified doctor to oversee the assessment, diagnosis and treatment of their illness giving rise to the foundation of contemporary psychiatry and the growth of the psychiatric profession. The involvement of psychiatry led to an expediential growth in the building of asylums as places where the ill could be detained and the latest scientific treatments used and evaluated

The power of psychiatry was further ratified by Acts of Parliament in 1828 and 1845 which gave the emerging profession almost exclusive rights to treat the insane. Other understandings of mental illness and non-medical methods of treatment were slowly but inexorably moved out of mainstream care.

This case study is different from a conventional case study in that it refers to the rise of a professional group who were trying to gain legitimacy and credibility for their work. Many of the techniques and methods used by the early psychiatrists would now be regarded as little more than 'quackery' based on false premises. Nonetheless, the ability to consistently appeal to rationalism and science aided the rise of psychiatry's professional status in the eyes of both the general public and the government. Horner (2009) similarly argues that the emerging social work profession sought to legitimise its existence in the

1920s through the adoption of theory and approaches from scientific disciplines such as psychology and psychiatry. It could of course be argued that that is still the case as social work increasingly appeals, or is forced to appeal, to evidence-based practice to legitimise its actions. In part, this appeal to evidence is the result of cases where practice has clearly failed, particularly with reference to young children, as demonstrated through serious case reviews and public inquiries across the range of practice contexts. Horner (2009), however, makes an interesting point in his review of the death in 1994 of Rikki Neave, a six-year-old child from Peterborough who was well known to the local authority and was on the 'at risk' register. That is, that the murder of children by those who are supposed to be looking after them can never be eradicated. Clearly, as a profession and as a society, we cannot afford to be fatalistic in our approach to child protection, and new procedures, better training and interagency co-operation must continue to evolve and improve. Nonetheless, it would be unwise to attempt to guarantee that no child will be killed in the future regardless of how much we claim that practice is based on sound evidence.

Optional further study

Manthorpe and Stanley (2004) provide an in-depth analysis of the role and influence of public inquiries in health and social care practice. While their analysis may be a little dated now, a significant strength is that it considers inquiries across a range of service user groups. On occasions, there is a danger that reviews of childcare cases take precedence over inquiries into practice in adult care. This book provides a welcome balance, particularly in its coverage of inquiries into abuse within learning difficulty.

The nature of evidence

Critical thinking exercise 1.3

Consider these contrasting quotations regarding evidence-based practice. Compile a list of key phrases within each definition and explore their meaning. Critically evaluate the usefulness of each definition.

> *Evidence-based practice is about finding, appraising and applying scientific evidence to the treatment and management of healthcare. Its ultimate goal is to support practitioners in their decision-making in order to eliminate the use of ineffective, inappropriate, too expensive and potentially dangerous practices.*
>
> **Hamer and Collinson** (1999: 6)

Evidence-based social care is the conscientious, explicit and judicious use of current best evidence in making decisions regarding the welfare of those in need.

Sheldon and Chilvers 2002, in **Smith** (2004: 8)

Hamer and Collinson (1999) are interpreting the debate from a health care perspective and consciously use the term 'scientific evidence'. They seem to favour an approach which systematically tests evidence with the view to using it to stamp out ineffective and costly practice. The definition deployed by Sheldon and Chilvers (2002) shares commonalities with the first definition but emphasises how evidence is used rather than where it comes from. This is an interesting difference to which we will return later in the chapter. While both of these definitions add to our understanding, neither attempts to offer a definition of what they mean by the term 'evidence'.

Key idea 1.1: **Evidence**

How we choose to define key terms such as evidence is obviously central to our discussion, and by no means easy. To return to an ongoing theme which reflects the scientific nature of our discussion so far, evidence is often viewed as information generated by the process of enquiry or research. For example, **SCIE** (2005: 16) suggest that

Evidence . . . is the product of research, defined as a form of structured enquiry capable of producing generalisable knowledge.

In a similar way to our previous definition by Hamer and Collinson (1999), this definition gives substance to the term evidence as it links it to 'structured enquiry' – a formal, planned and organised process which systematically produces knowledge which can then be usefully disseminated to a wider audience. This fits well with other authors who develop the argument further by suggesting that reliable evidence can *only* be produced via scientific research (Becker and Bryman 2004). This idea is further supported by Thompson and Thompson (2008) who argue that evidence is primarily generated by research techniques such as random controlled clinical trials which have a clear scientific rationale. They infer that the purpose behind the generation of this evidence is to uncover 'what works best' for the practitioner. While this may seem commonsensical it taps into the idea that 'hard' scientific evidence is of most use in guiding social work intervention. There is, however, an inherent danger within this assumption that sometimes practitioners and managers can 'become transfixed by the term evidence and the promise of a clear and single answer to difficult questions' (**Trinder** 2000: 154).

Science and scientific research also makes a number of other related assumptions: for example, the claim that facts or theories independently exist but can be discovered and understood via scientific enquiry. Consequently, facts are objective and have credence and credibility across a range of different contexts. To give a crude example, Isaac Newton 'discovered' the law of gravity in the seventeenth century. This law is applicable to all aspects of life and clearly existed independently and exerted an influence long before Newton 'discovered' it.

To summarise, our argument is that 'evidence' is a discrete term which contains a number of assumptions. Often it is assumed that evidence can only be produced by scientific research and that this evidence alone should form the basis of sound professional practice.

Key idea 1.2: **Knowledge**

'Knowledge', however, has a much more open meaning than evidence and, in the context of social work practice, is a complex, multifaceted concept. **Trevithick** (2007: 3) suggests that

> *knowledge involves gathering, analysing and synthesizing different theories (explanations) in order to arrive at some kind of tentative understanding, hypothesis or judgement.*

As you can see, this is a far less certain term which acknowledges both the potential inclusivity and the limitations of knowledge. The words, 'tentative' and 'hypothesis' seem to indicate that knowledge is only one component of the portfolio required by a social worker as they seek to understand a person or a situation. The author indicates that she is referring to theory or explanations. While the two are not indivisible the quote infers that knowledge needs to be scrutinised, not merely accepted, and put into practice as our previous discussion of evidence seemed to imply.

In their Knowledge Review for SCIE, Pawson and his colleagues state that

> *. . . social care knowledge is diverse and fragmented . . . and that . . . it would be easy to be selective and partisan in identifying and naming its crucial components.*
>
> **Pawson et al.** (2003: 4)

In other words, the scope, range and complexity of 'knowledge' means that any attempt to break it down or reduce it to a single-phrase definition may result in the exclusion of certain key elements. Nonetheless, some authors have attempted the task of defining at least some aspects of knowledge. Blom (2009), for example, suggests a fourfold typology that includes skills and factual knowledge, but then begins to widen the debate further by indicating that some components of knowledge are generated by experience and subjectivity. That is, the process of 'doing' and 'understanding' creates and adds to our knowledge. In other words, knowledge is 'made rather than revealed' (Taylor and White, 2000: 199). This is a crucial distinction for, as we have already suggested, traditional scientific research contradicts this position and implies that evidence is external and objective and can only be revealed through enquiry.

Key idea 1.3: **Can evidence or knowledge be regarded as true?**

The distinctions we have made between evidence and knowledge may be simplistic and open to critique, but they do helpfully lead to another key idea that we need to discuss regarding the nature of truth and validity. As we have argued, evidence seems a more certain term which at least hints that it may be true, while the claims made by knowledge seem less secure, less certain.

Critical thinking exercise 1.4

Do you think that evidence or knowledge can ever claim to be true? Or are they always open to amendment and reinterpretation?

We imagine that you have made a range of responses to these questions. Personally, we were reluctant to answer in the affirmative as there are many historical examples of knowledge or evidence that were clearly wrong. For example, the idea that the earth was flat was an accepted notion into the early decades of the nineteenth century before being disproved by astronomical research. In social policy there have been a number of pieces of legislation based on ideas or research that we would now regard as being far from the 'truth'. For example, the Mental Deficiency Act 1913 provided for the incarceration and segregation of people with learning difficulties, women who had given birth outside of marriage and alcoholics from the rest of society in order to prevent them from 'overbreeding'. This Act was at least partially based on evidence provided by the Eugenics Education Society that argued that Britain was being overrun and physically and morally impoverished by the children of genetically poor stock (Solway 1995). This latter example is useful as it demonstrates that sometimes evidence is contaminated by the prejudices and biases of the people who produce it and make claims on its behalf. Those people who felt that the population of Britain was being diminished by disabled people and 'moral degenerates' were unlikely to produce research evidence that contradicted their world view.

To address the second part of the question we return to Blom (2009) who argues that knowledge is always subjectively interpreted and presented and that our search for it is influenced by a range of elements such as our language, culture, context and assumptions. Knowledge therefore does not exist outside of our subjective interpretation of it and cannot be conceived as being truth. You will see that once again this stance undermines the notion that evidence is objective and exists independently. This is an important consideration for social workers working with a diverse range of people from different cultures and backgrounds. What we may perceive to be truth may be seen very differently by someone else. This argument is further exemplified by D'Cruz and Jones (2004) who suggest that the production of knowledge is inextricably linked to power and control. They give the example of colonisation where colonisers researched

> *... conquered peoples, their lives, practices and communities (which) were transformed into objects of knowledge by colonisers who created their own versions of knowledge and truth about colonised societies.*
>
> **D'Cruz and Jones** (2004: 52)

Wilson et al. (2008) appropriately summarise this argument in their discussion of the attributes of what they term 'social constructivist understandings of knowledge'. One of these is a disbelief in objectivity and

> *... a commitment to subjectivity as an inevitable, unavoidable, and necessary component of understanding.*
>
> **Wilson et al.** (2008: 97)

This argument then takes us even further away from an understanding of evidence or knowledge as being objective truth. Knowledge can only be gained and viewed through the prism of subjective interpretation. This subjectivity is not only unavoidable but should be embraced as a necessary component of the struggle to interpret and understand knowledge. The inherent subjectivity of evidence and knowledge then needs to be recognised. This, however, should not be seen as an excuse to discard the search for evidence and knowledge that underpins social work practice. On the contrary we must be open to emerging knowledge and be willing to adopt a questioning stance that recognises that our existing evidence base is never complete and that the search for knowledge is an ongoing quest. Despite these many questions and uncertainties, there are, however, a number of existing components of evidence and knowledge that we can recognise and which we need to examine.

Knowledge categorisation

Those of you who have been in education for some time will be used to theorists and academics attempting to devise categories in an attempt to provide their students with a systematic understanding of events or situations. On our bookshelf, for example, we have a well-thumbed copy of Emile Durkheim's (2002) *Le Suicide*, a classic nineteenth-century sociological study of suicide. Durkheim was one of the pioneers of sociological research and argued that the causes of suicide could be categorised into several types: egoistic, altruistic, and anomic suicide. On a more contemporary note, assessors and providers of social care services tend to group users into broad categories: children, learning disabled people, older people, mentally ill people and so on. Often these demarcation lines are used to allocate funding and resources and have a clear, practical use. Of course, it is not only social scientists and service providers who seek to categorise the world. Academics of all disciplines, organisations, governments and the 'ordinary person in the street' all make such attempts as categories are useful ways in which to collate and make sense of complex information. Categories, however, are rarely clear-cut or universally agreed upon by all who use them and are often subject to challenge and critique.

Different ways of categorising knowledge in social work

It might be expected then that defining the different types or categories of knowledge that inform professional social work practice could also be complex. Trevithick (2007) has written about the many attempts to provide social care with a schema of knowledge, and comments that

> *. . . different authors have sought to find ways to classify the knowledge base of social work and to place an emphasis on certain features over others. This is a dense jungle of concepts, often deploying rather sterile terms to describe these different features.*
>
> **Trevithick** (2007: 1216)

Bearing these reservations in mind, in this section we introduce you to a number of different ways in which writers have considered how best to categorise those elements of knowledge and evidence which they see as underpinning professional practice. The first approach highlights the fact that categorising knowledge itself is not a value-free or unbiased activity. Trevithick (2007) argues that there is a dichotomy between two common approaches which seek to classify knowledge. The first approach rests on the ideological assumption that systematically produced scientific knowledge provides the best foundation for practice. You have already been introduced to this argument and will recognise the second assumption identified by Trevithick that knowledge which is deemed to be objective and rational will be given credence over less rigorous forms of knowledge.

Trevithick uses a quotation from another writer to exemplify how this type of knowledge may be didactically seen to operate in social care:

> *. . . if research findings indicate approach B is the most effective with problem A, and problem A is the one confronted by the practitioner, then approach B should be adopted.*
>
> **Sheppard et al.** (2000: 466–7)

The underlying assumption within this view is that research is the most effective way to generate knowledge, which in turn could lead to a rigid, formal approach to practice. This approach, however, has obvious limitations as it does not reflect the fluidity and complexity of the situations typically faced by the social care professional, or the multi-faceted nature of intervention.

In contrast, the second approach to categorisation outlined by Trevithick emphasises that knowledge needs to be put into practice in order for it to be welded and adapted until it is fit for purpose. In other words, there is an ideological value placed on knowledge generated by action and 'doing'. Due to the sheer unpredictability of the task, the social worker cannot simply apply rigid rules and formulae; they must wrestle with a range of different knowledge in

order to acquire an in-depth understanding of what is happening, and why and how best to address these concerns.

Trevithick (2007: 1216)

Crucially, this second approach values and promotes the desirability of understanding why something is happening and the ability to gauge what needs to be done using knowledge honed and validated by experience. We are sure that you will realise that this argument echoes the previously discussed approach of Blom (2009), who suggests that knowledge is made, rather than revealed.

The difference between these two approaches to categorisation is sometimes overstated and we need to acknowledge that many of the concepts we will be discussing in this chapter are, to borrow a sociological concept from Max Weber, 'ideal types'. That is, they describe idealised versions of what actually happens in practice. In reality, few attempts to generate knowledge will fall exclusively into the 'science' or 'experience' arena.

Knowledge classification according to mode of production

The distinctions identified by Trevithick are paralleled by McLaughlin (2007), who moves away from a consideration of underpinning value perspectives to explore how knowledge is produced or gained. McLaughlin cites the work of Gibbons et al. (1994) in outlining two distinctive methods by which knowledge might be created and thus offers two categories by which we can distinguish or separate different types of knowledge. These methods are labelled as 'mode 1' and 'mode 2'.

The methods by which knowledge is generated in mode 1 mirror the 'scientific' ideological underpinnings identified by Trevithick (2007) as it is, to generalise, academic knowledge produced, owned and consumed by the academic community. The pursuit of knowledge itself is deemed to be of prime significance and scientific methods are used to generate and verify knowledge.

Knowledge produced by mode 2, however, equates to Trevithick's second category of knowledge which values the primary role of experience and application. Mode 2 knowledge is produced primarily 'in the field' by practitioners who may come from a range of disciplinary backgrounds. The knowledge produced can often be of relevance to a range of settings and is likely to be generated and 'owned' by a range of participants. For example, in social work research it is claimed that the research process is often more democratic than in laboratory-based scientific research and may incorporate contributions from service users, carers, practitioners and academic staff (Hardwick and Worsley 2011) Social work, unlike many mainstream non-professional academic disciplines, is rarely concerned with the production of knowledge purely for its own sake. On the contrary, it seeks to produce knowledge which will actively assist practitioners to deal with the practicalities of professional intervention. In other words, the knowledge produced by social work research seeks to have a practical outcome. To quote **McLaughlin** (2007: 144):

The primary purpose of social work research is to promote and develop effective social work practice.

This distinction between how knowledge is produced is purely one way that types of knowledge can be classified. We now move on to consider a third method of categorising knowledge.

Knowledge classification according to its source

In 2002 SCIE, whose role it is to identify, enhance and disseminate the knowledge base for good practice in social care, commissioned a team of researchers *to explore the types and quality of social care knowledge* **Pawson et al**. (2003: vii).

In the Knowledge Review subsequently produced for SCIE, Pawson et al. (2003) argue that it is neither the value perspective which underpins the classification of knowledge (Trevithick) nor how the knowledge is generated (McLaughlin) that is of significance, but the sources from which it comes.

SCIE's recommended typology of knowledge that informs professional practice has five categories or 'source domains'. These are:

Organisational knowledge such as that which is gained from organisations, through the management, oversight and governance of social care;

Practitioner knowledge which arises from the experience, practice wisdom, tacit knowledge and reflective practice of those engaged in social care practice. This would include direct practitioner research;

Policy community knowledge that arises from the wider strategic and policy environment. This would include institutional reviews, audits, commissions and 'think tank' outputs;

Research knowledge 'gathered systematically with predetermined design' and including empirical inquiries, evaluations and evaluative reports;

User and Carer knowledge which arises directly from the experience and reflections of service users.

Pawson et al. (2003)

Critical thinking exercise 1.5

We have provided three examples of how knowledge can be classified, although we have been careful not to overly critique these attempts. What do you think are the strengths and weaknesses of these different approaches? Do you think that one approach is any better than the others?

Here is our response to this exercise.

Knowledge classification according to ideological underpinning (Trevithick 2007)

Strengths	Draws attention to the important role of values and ideology
Weaknesses	Accentuates the distinction between science and experience Does not examine how knowledge is generated

Knowledge classification according to the mode of production (McLaughlin 2007)

Strengths	Provides a clear rationale for social work research
Weaknesses	Accentuates the distinction between science and experience Does not examine how knowledge is generated

Knowledge classification according to source (Pawson et al. 2003)

Strengths	Pragmatic, comprehensive, has clear practical usage, and is accessible
Weaknesses	Does not examine how or why knowledge is generated

You may well have produced a more comprehensive answer to the questions posed. In many ways the weaknesses we have included could as easily be seen as being strengths. Is it a failing that theorists articulate the clear distinctions that exist between scientific methods of producing knowledge and those which are borne out of experience? Both methods have their place in social care and some would say that the differences that exist are not insurmountable. Equally, we need to acknowledge that the respective authors set out not so much to provide a comprehensive understanding of the whole process of developing ideas, producing and disseminating knowledge, more a thoughtful explanation of different aspects of the process. You may think, purely through the weight of numbers in the strengths column, that we particularly favour the final approach of Pawson et al. (2003). This is not necessarily the case as we would argue that we need to have an appreciation of what underpins and guides the production of knowledge and not simply be able to name the source from which it derives. Consequently, we suggest that all three approaches enhance our understanding and need to be considered together.

Chapter Summary

In this chapter you were presented with a number of key debates. The first question raised the issue, 'what underpins social work?' As we saw, some suggest that social work practice is purely commonsensical and dependent on good interpersonal skills. While accepting the need for both of these attributes we refuted this notion by highlighting the reasons why practice should be underpinned by both evidence and knowledge. We then began to tease out the key differences between 'evidence' and 'knowledge'. You should now be aware that there are some crucial distinctions between these two commonly used terms and of the need to be cautious as to how we use them.

The next key debate considered if either evidence or knowledge could be viewed as being entirely reliable and valid. In otherwords, is it true? We presented a number of positions but argued that the way we understand, interpret and filter knowledge is essentially a subjective process. Consequently, we need to be vigilant about simplistically accepting knowledge as a robust basis for practice; the search for knowledge is never complete or fully realised.

The chapter was summarised by briefly considering the categorisation of knowledge. Again, we invited you to consider that this is not a straightforward activity and that there are ideologies and value positions that underlie any attempt to group or classify. You may have also noted that we increasingly used the term *knowledge* and decreasingly used the term *evidence* as the chapter evolved. To a large extent, this was a conscious decision as we feel that knowledge, with all its uncertainties and ambiguities, is a more helpful term to use when considering social work practice. You may of course disagree but we hope that you will enjoy the continuing debate over the rest of this book.

While some of these conceptual ideas and debates are challenging we hope that you can see how this process is beginning to develop your critical thinking skills. Specifically you

- reflected on the reasons why social work requires knowledge and evidence to underpin the tasks that it does (skill 1);
- analysed the differences and commonalities between the key terms 'evidence' and 'knowledge' (skills 2, 3 and 4);
- reflected on the question, 'is evidence and knowledge "true" or does it need to be constantly reviewed and refined?' (skill 3);
- examined how and why knowledge is categorised and the ideology that underpins this process (skill 2).

Building on these skills is important and we hope that you will find our material both stimulating and challenging. The aim of the book is to incrementally add to your ability to critically analyse issues as your reading progresses.

In the next chapter we begin to critically consider the basis of knowledge. In particular, we will take one of the categorisations that we have discussed, that of Pawson et al. (2003), as a starting point for a critical analysis of the different elements of knowledge which underpin social work practice. This debate will be expansive and will build on many of the themes identified in this first chapter.

Further reading

Pawson, R., Boaz, A., Grayson, L., Long, A. and Barnes, C. (2003) *Types and Quality of Knowledge in Social Care.* Knowledge Review 3. London: SCIE.

This 'knowledge review' from the Social Care Institute for Excellence identifies the main types of research, experience and wisdom that combine to form the social care knowledge base. This review has been drawn upon in the later part of this chapter and forms the underpinning basis for the structure of the following chapter in this book, so accessing this text would help you to further your understanding of key concepts discussed in the first part of this book. The review is freely downloadable from **www.scie.org.uk**

Trevithick, P. (2008) Revisiting the Knowledge Base of Social Work: A Framework for Practice. *British Journal of Social Work*, 38: 1212–37.

Trevithick argues that social work practice is a highly skilled activity that calls for an extensive knowledge base. This journal article debates differing perspectives on what constitutes the knowledge base of social work, and develops a framework that locates the knowledge that service users and carers bring to the encounter with the same standing as the knowledge demonstrated by the professionals.

Trinder, L. and Reynolds, S. (2000) (eds) *Evidence-Based Practice: A Critical Appraisal.* Oxford: Blackwell Publishing.

This edited book takes a broad look at the notion of 'evidence-based practice' across a range of disciplinary areas, and in doing so supports the debates about concepts, challenges and perceptions that have been commenced in this chapter.

2 Where does the knowledge that influences practice come from?

Ian Mathews

Achieving a Social Work Degree

Exercises in this chapter will focus on

- skill 2 comparing and contrasting different viewpoints and experiences
- skill 4 evaluating different perspectives and ideas
- skill 7 reflection

In addition its content is particularly relevant to the following Social Work Subject Benchmarks.

4.7 the ability to acquire and apply the habits of critical reflection, self-evaluation and consultation, and make appropriate use of research in decision-making about practice and in the evaluation of outcomes

5.1.2 the ability to understand the location of contemporary social work within historical, comparative and global perspectives

5.1.4 the ability to acquire and apply knowledge and critical appraisal of relevant social research and evaluation methodologies, and the evidence base for social work

Introduction

In this chapter we continue to analyse the knowledge foundations of social work practice and extend our debate regarding the categorisation of knowledge. As discussed in the previous chapter, attempting to divide knowledge into categories is not a straightforward task as 'knowledge' itself is a contested term. Equally, given the complexities of social work and the breadth of knowledge required to undertake the task, it is perhaps not surprising that typologies and systems of categorisation often appear to be unsatisfactory. You may recall that we alluded in Chapter 1 to the concept of 'ideal types' devised by Max Weber (1864–1920), one of the nineteenth-century founding fathers of sociology. An ideal type is an idealised description which draws on the key characteristics and attributes of the phenomenon being studied, but does not necessarily describe reality. To an extent, the categories and divisions within knowledge we discuss can be seen as ideal types as they are idealised descriptions and not discrete entities. Each category influences, and in turn is influenced by, the other categories. For example, practitioner knowledge (also known as practice wisdom) is essentially knowledge generated by the experience of doing the task. Nonetheless, this form of knowledge is shaped by a range of other categories of knowledge, such as the influence of policy and legislation, the knowledge of the service user and the contribution of research.

The building blocks of social work knowledge

In the previous chapter we began to explore the differences and commonalities between the contested terms 'knowledge' and 'evidence' and briefly analysed some of the ways in which they could be categorised. In this chapter we want to build on those arguments by using the fivefold typology devised by Pawson et al. (2003) as a vehicle to analyse the foundations of social work knowledge. The reason for choosing this typology is pragmatic, based on the fact that it incorporates a 'good enough' range of different types of knowledge. As we hope you will realise from your reading of Chapter 1, this is not to suggest that it is without ideological bias or that it does not contain assumptions that you might wish to contest.

Pawson et al. (2003) implicitly divide knowledge into two broad themes: 'informal' knowledge which is generated through the personal experience of either providing or receiving social work support; and more 'formal' knowledge which is generated by academic research or by organisations which manage or provide services. It is our intention to devote more time to analysing informal knowledge as more formal aspects of knowledge production will be explored later in the book.

The first three categories of knowledge we will be considering, practitioner knowledge, service user knowledge and carer knowledge, implicitly raise a profound question which has a number of implications. For the existence and use of these more informal sources of knowledge question the idea that objectivity is always a necessary prerequisite characteristic of knowledge. If knowledge based on subjective experience is equally valid and useful as evidence produced by more 'scientific' processes it calls into question attempts to produce hierarchies of knowledge. As has already been noted in Chapter 1, scientifically produced knowledge is often viewed as being the best type of knowledge due to its perceived rigour and objectivity. Exponents of this view would perhaps acknowledge that other forms of knowledge have their place but that they will always be inferior to science. Our contention throughout this book is that this is not always the case and that informal knowledge plays a key role in informing social work practice.

Practitioner knowledge

We want to start our analysis by initially concentrating on the contested idea of practitioner knowledge. In order to engage in the debate surrounding this term, we would like you to complete the following exercise.

Critical thinking exercise 2.1

Write down your own definition of 'practitioner knowledge'. Do not worry if you are unclear what the term means as sometimes engaging in a task and then reflecting on it is a good way to learn.

There are a number of definitions of practitioner knowledge but perhaps the obvious place to start is with the one provided by **Pawson et al.** (2003: 49)

> *Practitioner knowledge is acquired directly through the practice of social caring and the distillation of collective wisdom at many points through media such as education and training, requesting and receiving advice, attending team meetings and case conferences, and comparing notes.*

From this definition we can deduce that this type of knowledge derives directly from the experience of social work practice, working over time with service users from similar backgrounds experiencing similar issues, and the gaining and sharing of 'collective wisdom' with colleagues. The inclusion of the word wisdom is significant as the phrases 'practitioner knowledge' and 'practice wisdom' are often used coterminously. There is, however, a danger that the 'wisdom' referred to is sometimes based on little more than personal anecdote, pragmatism, and at worst, poor practice. As we noted in the previous chapter regarding the term common sense, what might be wisdom to one practitioner could be little more than foolishness to another. **O'Sullivan** (2005: 222) captures these concerns in one of his descriptions of practice wisdom as being

> *. . . unreliable, personal, idiosyncratic knowledge built up through practice experience.*

Other attempts to define practitioner knowledge are equally elusive. Rolfe et al. (2001) talk about practice wisdom as the implicit ability to 'know how' to undertake a task or approach a service user. Similarly, Wilson et al. (2008: 104–5) offer a number of possible terms to describe intuition such as 'gut feelings', 'innate gifts' and the ability to be unconsciously aware of other people's emotions or the environmental context of the situation. As these brief quotations demonstrate, it can be difficult to articulate exactly what is meant by practice wisdom or to quantify the value of knowledge gained through experience. This, we would suggest, is especially the case in a culture which values (even overvalues) rational thought, logic and the rigour of scientific explanation. Nonetheless, we will argue that practice wisdom and other sources of informal knowledge have an important contribution to make to effective social work practice.

As part of a wider debate we need to acknowledge that professions allied to social work similarly recognise and increasingly value the contribution of practitioner knowledge. For example, Gilgun (2005) in her discussion of practitioner knowledge in medicine argues that practice based solely on rational knowledge is deficient because it fails to

> *. . . recognise the uncertainty and ambiguity inherent in clinical practice and research evidence.*
>
> **Gilgun** (2005: 54)

Drawing on the work of Epstein (1999) she suggests that 'mindful practice' which incorporates empathy, compassion and altruism coupled with an understanding of the cultural and religious values of both physician and patient provides a better basis for decision-making. In other words, the doctor/patient relationship and the clinical decisions that define the relationship are driven by a complex range of factors. Some are based on the traditional basis of medicine such as clinical research and science, while others recognise the more implicit nature of experience and context. You will note that this argument, coming as it does from the medical profession, stands in contrast to many of the comments that we made about the status of science in Chapter 1. If medicine is recognising the value of knowledge that stands outside of its traditional and formally constructed evidence base then surely social work needs to do the same.

This emphasis on the significance of the person behind the role moves the definition of practitioner knowledge forward as it highlights the importance of *personal* experience, as opposed to traditional definitions which concentrate on knowledge deriving from *professional* training. Wilson et al. (2008) argue that knowledge which derives from personal experience is important as it may assist the social worker to better understand service user' or carers' perspectives. They use the example of a student who has a disabled sibling and suggest that this could be a valuable source of knowledge deriving as it does from lived experience. We need, however, to exercise caution when using knowledge based on personal experience as self-awareness, personal values and the recognition of difference and diversity are essential if subjective views are to promote and not hinder good practice. O'Sullivan (2005), for example, suggests that there is a requirement for social workers to continually question and reflect on their interpretations, especially if built on personal experience, as there is an inherent danger that we accept information that confirms our viewpoint while simultaneously ignoring contra indicators.

To return to Gilgun (2005), she argues that doctors, as they gain experience, move away from overtly rational and analytical practice and adopt an interpretative process which filters differing kinds of evidence including intuition, past experience, and personal/professional values. Her thinking broadly corresponds with the five-staged model of expertise development devised by Dreyfus and Dreyfus (1986) which we now want to briefly consider.

Research summary

Professional development and the use of practitioner knowledge

The **Dreyfus and Dreyfus** (1986) model of expertise development is now over 20 years old and has been subject to a number of criticisms. Nonetheless, it offers an interesting view on the sequential development of professional expertise and the use of intuition. An adapted version of the model suggests that the professional gains intuitive expertise over time and that this facet of knowledge becomes an increasingly important guide to practice.

The stages identified are:

Novice the beginning professional rigidly follows taught rules. They demonstrate only limited awareness of the context and do not use their own discretion.

Advanced beginner the professional begins to develop a basic awareness of the context of decision-making but continues to regard each piece of information separately and as having equal merit.

Competent the learner is able to manage competing demands and conflicting information. They develop an ability to plan ahead and adopt a longer-term view.

Proficient the worker develops a holistic understanding of situations and is able to prioritise competing information. They can identify deviations from the norm and consequently are able to make quicker decisions.

Expert the expert intuitively knows what to do and is no longer dependent on taught rules or maxims.

If we apply this model to practice there is an obvious weakness to the final stage of this process as social work is so complex and process driven that no professional could ever solely rely on intuition. It would potentially be a very dangerous and illegal stance to adopt. Given the legislative and policy framework that contextualises social work, no worker is going to be in a position to ignore the 'rules' that govern practice. Even so, this model offers a glimpse into the way in which practitioner knowledge becomes increasingly important as professionals become more confident in their skills and experienced in their role.

Critical thinking exercise 2.2

Having thought a little more about practitioner knowledge revisit your initial definition and reflect on the issues raised so far in this chapter.

To summarise the debate within this section of Chapter 2, practitioner knowledge can be a useful aide to practice, especially if used in a reflective way which acknowledges its inherent limitations. As we have argued, practice can be informed by such insights but it can never solely guide professional action. The main criticisms of practitioner knowledge are that it is highly subjective. Consequently, it can be difficult to confirm or refute and it is not always built on reliable foundations. Nonetheless, both social work and other professions recognise the value of practice wisdom and it does have a part to play in practice. With these thoughts in mind, we now want to turn to another form of knowledge which is equally contested and open to critique.

Service user and carer knowledge

We want to commence this section of the chapter by opening a critical debate. In many areas of social work, including academic literature, policy-making and legislation, the generic term 'service users and carers' is frequently used. This is especially the case when representation or input is sought by service providers regarding the planning and evaluation of services. While there are sometimes good reasons why these groups of people should be considered together this is not always the case.

Critical thinking exercise 2.3

Ignoring the fact that it is of course possible to be both a carer and a user of services, make a list of the differences between service users and carers.

At first sight, this may seem a simplistic task but a critical engagement with the question reveals a number of key differences. For example, you may have noted that there is a difference of perspective. Service users have first-hand 'lived experience' and knowledge of using services as well as an in-depth knowledge of their own personal situation. As such they have unique expertise to offer and a significant contribution to make to the social care debate.

Carers of course may be able to contribute additional knowledge to this perspective but often they have a different viewpoint to share. Their expertise arises from providing care and support to the person they care for and undertaking all the other tasks and responsibilities that carers do. The person they care for may receive services intended to meet the needs of their carers, but carers themselves rarely receive direct service provision. We appreciate that this point is increasingly contentious but in the main, service provision is targeted at the needs of service users.

Another key difference is that of aspiration. The needs and wishes of service users and their carers are often different, even to the extent of being, at times, in direct competition to one another. The relationship between service users and carers is a complex and dynamic one and we must be careful not to make general assumptions. Nonetheless, we need to recognise that sometimes it is necessary to separately consider the needs, wishes and contributions of service users and carers and not uncritically treat them as being one and the same. It is our argument that when we consider the knowledge that underpins social work, service users and carers have different insights and strengths to offer.

Service user knowledge

As we have already suggested, some forms of knowledge are traditionally viewed as being better than others. Typically, those areas of knowledge that are seen to be intuitive or based on experience are seen as being less valid than those built on research or scientific explanation. This criticism has been made against service user and carer knowledge, as well as practitioner knowledge (Beresford 2000; Wilson et al. 2008). An obvious feature of all of these types of knowledge is that they derive from professional or personal life experience and are subjective in nature. In a sense we could say that they positively reject scientific objectivity and celebrate the value of subjective/partisan knowledge. This is particularly true of a number of service user organisations which have contributed to knowledge production in social work and have explicitly critiqued the accepted academic way of conducting research which emphasises 'neutrality' and 'distance' from the subject being researched. By definition, research produced by service users and carers has a very different perspective and purpose from academic research. We return to this argument on a number of occasions but for now we simply recognise that often a considerable disparity exists.

Research summary

Glasby and Beresford (2006) in their influential paper on evidence-based practice articulate a number of reasons why the experiences and world view of service users has often been distorted or denied in formal academic research.

1. Academic research is flawed due to the unequal power relations that exist between researchers and those who they study (often service users). Research results often reflect this imbalance and the understandings and experiences of service users are either inaccurately portrayed or used in a paternalistic manner.
2. Structural factors such as class, race, age, gender and other forms of difference interfere with the process and interpretation of knowledge generation.
3. The ideological bias and value positions of researchers reduce their ability to value the person or the experience they are researching.
4. Discriminatory models used in research, such as the medical model of mental illness, tend to subordinate and pathologise service users. This in turn marginalises the knowledge and experience of service users.

adapted from **Glasby and Beresford** (2006: 274)

A common theme expressed within this critique is the evident disparity in power between well-paid university-based researchers and those who are the subjects of their research, which can lead to discrepancy and distortion. We could reflect that frequently in practice there is a similar power divide between service users and social workers (Smith 2008). This in turn may mean that the difficulty academics have in interpreting and valuing the contribution of service users is mirrored by a similar lack of understanding by social workers in practice. In passing, we may note that hierarchies of power, where one person or profession or way of working is deemed to be 'better' or more important than another, impacts on many aspects of health and social care. For example, Johnstone (2009), reviewing her experience of working as a clinical psychologist for over 25 years in the mental health system, notes that non-psychiatric viewpoints or ways of working are consistently ignored or devalued by consultant psychiatrists as being less important than the work of psychiatry. This is an interesting observation as it reminds us of our recurring debate concerning the value of different types of knowledge.

Critical thinking exercise 2.4

Revisit the case study we used in Chapter 1 concerning the growth of psychiatry in the nineteenth century and reflect on the contemporary comments by Johnstone. What do they tell us about the way that psychiatry has viewed and continues to view alternative understandings of mental health?

You may reflect that little seems to have changed in the way that psychiatry has defended its position of dominance in the treatment of mentally ill people. A valuable weapon used by psychiatry has been its claim that it is founded on the most reliable forms of knowledge: rationality and a scientific evidence base. Conversely, other competing understandings of mental illness, such as the social model or spirituality, often seem to have a less scientific knowledge base on which to stake their claim.

Optional further study

There are a number of chapters in **Reynolds et al.** (2009) which talk about the importance of recognising alternative understandings and knowledge within the mental health system.

For example, Chapter 4 by **Wright et al.** discusses the inhuman way that people with personality disorder are often treated in psychiatric care and how staff understandings of complex conditions contribute to this inhumanity.

Chapter 2 by **Leach** provides a good basic account of the different approaches that exist defining mental health and distress.

To return to our main discussion regarding the role of service user knowledge we want to argue that the intuitive knowledge that service users bring with them is an essential building block to effective social work practice. For example, Trivedi (2009) argues that the understanding of who the person is and how they choose to define themselves provides a unique contribution to the social worker–service user relationship. She suggests that on occasions this knowledge is disregarded, or not even sought, by professionals. Consequently the identity of service users is subverted by the assumptions made and language used by professionals and systems. She gives the personal example of being formally described as being a 'non-white', which implies that 'whiteness' is the norm against which all other colours and ethnicities are judged. While this example may be contentious the message it conveys, that personal definitions and perceptions are not of significance, cannot be ignored.

This poor practice is pithily observed by Ron Coleman, a well-known mental health survivor:

> *In the early 1980s I was diagnosed as schizophrenic. By 1990 that was changed to chronic schizophrenia and in 1993 I gave up being a schizophrenic and decided to be Ron Coleman.*
>
> **Coleman** (1999:2)

It may seem an obvious point that we need to start with how a service user sees themselves and the knowledge they bring of their own situation but this element of understanding often seems to be disregarded. For example, Wells (2009) relates how she has had continual battles with mental health practitioners regarding her type of medication. Insisting that her knowledge of herself and the way her body responds to medication often seemed to go unheard by practitioners. Similarly, Branfield and Beresford (2006) provide a comprehensive list of missed opportunities for service providers and professionals who do not make the best use of service user knowledge in evaluating and planning services, arranging care packages and working with people on a one-to-one basis.

These missed opportunities stand in contrast to examples of good practice where service user knowledge is valued and used as a means of promoting real change. Dickens and Woodfield (2004), for example, in their report on an innovative project to tackle youth homelessness in London, suggest that an explicit recognition of young people's understandings of why they were in crisis and an approach that emphasised involvement and consultation were significant factors in the success of the project. The mutual understanding generated by this approach led to the provision of packages of support that enabled young people to address the underlying problems that had led them to a point of crisis. In passing, we might also note the benefit of consistent, one-to-one support being provided by the same key worker. This consistency cannot always be provided but assists the worker to develop knowledge of the user while simultaneously building up a relationship which enables the user to share increasing amounts of knowledge about themselves to the worker.

Optional further study

If you want to explore further some of the challenges and opportunities presented by the participation of service users and carers, we recommend that you read 'Service user and carer participation in social work' by **Warren** (2007). In particular, Chapter 3 provides an accessible discussion of the differences that exist between the rhetoric of health and social care organisations and the realities faced by service users.

Carer knowledge

The final element of subjective knowledge that we want to discuss in this chapter is carer knowledge. That is the 'wisdom', expertise and knowledge gained from the task of caring for another person. This type of knowledge should not be underestimated or ignored for

> *The 'apparent ordinariness' of care is deceptive and can often hide sophisticated, highly skilled and much valued approaches to personal and social support.*

Beresford (2008: 1)

To this we may add that the knowledge that derives from the caring task is often multifaceted and detailed in nature. While formal carers, those who are employed to provide care services, often have knowledge which can be invaluable to the social work practitioner, we want to concentrate on informal carers: family, friends and neighbours who provide care often without remuneration or recognition. We will return to this theme later in the book as it is sometimes a source of knowledge which professionals choose to overlook.

Critical thinking exercise 2.5

Make a list of the different areas of knowledge that informal carers may be able to contribute to a social work assessment.

It is likely that the principal component of knowledge that a carer will possess will be about the person they are caring for and the joint needs that are generated by the caring relationship.

Research summary

Twigg and Atkin (1994) provide a summary of some of the knowledge that carers may possess.

Physical tending – knowledge about how to go about caring for a person. The best way 'to do things', how to avoid confrontation and how to work around restrictions. This knowledge may be practical in nature, such as how to use a hoist or empty a stoma bag. Equally, it may relate to the emotional, sexual, or physical needs of the cared-for person.

Behavioural difficulties – some carers develop considerable expertise in 'how to handle' the person they are caring for. Sometimes people with mental health problems, cognitive impairment, or learning difficulty may display aggressive or unpredictable behaviours. Over time, carers come to understand the triggers behind this behaviour and can become experts in diffusing such difficulties.

Restrictedness – the isolation and lack of opportunity that often accompany the role of carer. This can include lack of opportunity to socialise, go on holiday or find employment. This knowledge relates more to the emotional impact of caring and is especially useful in sharing with other carers.

Information – carers gain expertise in finding and disseminating information and navigating their way round health and social care systems. They develop specialist knowledge of the different services offered by different agencies and are able to pass on their knowledge to other carers.

adapted from **Twigg and Atkin** (1994: 31–48)

This list represents no more than a snapshot of some of the areas of knowledge that a carer may be able to contribute to social work practice. There are many more that you may have been able to identify. The first two areas are self-explanatory and there are obvious ways in which knowledge about the personal care needs of the service user and how to avoid or minimise risk arising from behavioural problems is useful to assessment.

The other two areas of knowledge, the experience of restrictedness and information gathering, are of importance to formal assessment. After all, a holistic assessment should take into account emotional needs and recognise the demands placed on both carer and service user by the proximity and interdependency of their relationship. An assessment should also be an opportunity to gauge how much a carer knows about services within the area and what further information they require.

These areas of knowledge, however, have a clear usage beyond contributing to a formal assessment in the way that such knowledge can be shared to inform the work undertaken by other carers. We might reflect that one of the benefits of these more subjective types of knowledge is that they often have a direct practical application which assists others to improve their awareness.

We also need to be clear that there is a danger when we label practitioners, service users or carers 'experts by experience' that we do not automatically assume that their knowledge is either complete or entirely reliable. As with all elements of subjectivity, there are gaps, omissions and errors which need to be recognised. For example, Osmond et al. (2008) in their study of experienced foster carers in Australia found that carers were knowledgeable about some aspects of underpinning theory and knowledge relating to childcare but were less familiar with other significant concepts. For example, they misunderstood nuances around 'attachment' and 'did not have recourse to a deep understanding of abuse related knowledge' (asmond et al. 2008: 269). Given the nature of their role and the depth of experience they had this is worrying but maybe not surprising. Even the most committed and knowledgeable carer cannot be expected to know everything about the carer's task.

To summarise, so far in this chapter we have provided an introductory discussion of the 'informal' categories of knowledge that underpin the practice of social work as defined by Pawson et al. (2003). Later in this book we will return to analyse these aspects of knowledge in different ways – so please treat these initial explorations as a starting point. We now turn to those categories of knowledge which are identified by Pawson et al. (2003) as being more 'formal' in nature. That is to say, knowledge which is formally created by academics or organisations involved in the planning and delivery of social care. As stated in the introduction to this chapter, we will work our way quickly through these types of more formal knowledge as they are reviewed on a number of occasions throughout this book.

Policy community knowledge

Pawson et al. (2003) define this type of knowledge as emanating from bodies such as central government, local government, audits, reviews, commissions and 'think tanks'. This knowledge is often created by an amalgam of public servants, politicians, legal experts, managers, academics and increasingly service users who work together to produce policy and procedure to inform and guide service provision. On occasions it may comprise a set of recommendations in response to failings in a particular case. For example, in the aftermath of the death of Baby Peter (Connelly) in 2007, Lord Laming published a review of child protection services entitled, *The Protection of Children in England: A Progress Report* (Laming 2009). On other occasions it may be produced to highlight new legislation or ways of working, or simply to better inform the task of social work. This type of knowledge is pivotal to social work practice and it often forms the backcloth to intervention.

An example of how policy community knowledge informs social work practice

In order to demonstrate the diverse nature of this type of knowledge we will explore the Social Care Institute for Excellence (SCIE) (2004a) research briefing number seven: 'Assessing and diagnosing Attention Deficit Hyperactivity Disorder (ADHD)' which is available at **www.scie.org.uk**. Those of you who are familiar with the work of SCIE will remember that the purpose of their research briefings is to provide a concise summary of research and knowledge which can inform the social work task.

In this research briefing they list a number of sources of knowledge which they have used to compile the document. Included in the section entitled 'Policy community knowledge' is

- a guide from the World Health Organization; an organisational arm of the United Nations which co-ordinates advice on global health matters;
- a report from the Department for Education and Skills and the Mental Health Foundation; respectively a UK Government department and a charity;
- a pathway to assist in the diagnosis and assessment of ADHD from the Scottish Intercollegiate Guidelines Network; a body which develops evidence-based clinical practice guidelines for the National Health Service in Scotland;
- reference to the role of the clinical health professional in diagnosis taken from The National Institute for Health and Clinical Excellence (NICE), the health service equivalent to SCIE, which is responsible for providing national guidance on the promotion of good health and the prevention and treatment of ill health in the UK.

As can be seen, the diversity of the sources used by SCIE is interesting as it highlights the commonality between many government, health and social care agencies and the holistic connection between health and social care. All of the agencies mentioned have an active interest in disseminating information and guidance which promotes good practice. Equally, all have different perspectives to offer and different biases within their advice. For example, the government agencies have a quasi-independent role but are subject to political control. The United Nations has a global perspective to offer while the Mental Health Foundation is much more interested in promoting the voice and interests of service users within the UK. All of these examples however come from within the policy community.

Organisational knowledge

The second type of formal knowledge described by Pawson et al. (2003) is that gained by organisations through the management, oversight and governance of social care. This knowledge is generated and often disseminated by managers, senior executives and politicians who are responsible for the provision of social care services. Often it details the conduct expected of staff in delivering services and sets out standards and targets to be met. There is a clear interplay between this type of knowledge and policy community knowledge. To generalise, organisational knowledge puts into practice the guidance issued by policymakers at a higher level and provides a local interpretation of national policy. It principally concerns itself with regulation, compliance and the meeting of set standards. Consequently it provides and prescribes the context for the delivery of local social care services.

Both of these latter types of knowledge provide the socio-political and organisational context for professional practice. In an increasingly bureaucratic world seemingly dominated by targets, objectives and performance indicators, social workers clearly need to have knowledge of this context. Nonetheless, practitioners also need to retain the independence of mind to critically evaluate such policy contexts and challenge new initiatives if they appear to compromise the values of social work practice.

Research knowledge

The final form of knowledge we want to consider is that of research community knowledge. That is, knowledge which is generated by academic enquiry or 'field' research undertaken by practitioners, service users or carers. A critical discussion of the role of research in social work and ways in which practitioners and service users may understand, deploy and conduct research will be the focus of a later chapter in this book. Consequently, in this chapter we will confine ourselves to an introductory discussion concerning the sometimes fraught relationship between research and social work practice. It could be argued that it has always been envisaged that social work should have a close relationship with research, with its activities and outcomes being guided and informed by research findings. In order to substantiate this claim, we need to briefly consider the historical evolution of social work and the intention to embed research into practice.

Research summary

Horner (2009: 88) traces the emergence of the social work profession and notes the comments made in 1903 by those reviewing the work of the 'Charity Organisation Society', one of the many voluntary organisations that pre-dated and guided the evolution of professional social work. In the review it unequivocally stated that social work practice 'must be made scientific'. This early emphasis is telling as it highlights the Victorian/Edwardian veneration of disciplines such as medicine which seemed to offer a cure for the ills of society with their use of science and rationalism. In the same year the Charity founded the School of Sociology in London, a precursor to the London School of Economics (LSE), with the aim of equipping practitioners with grounding in social theory and law. It is perhaps not coincidental that one of the founders of contemporary social work, Dame Eileen Younghusband (1902–81), was subsequently both a student and an academic at the LSE. At the birth of statutory social work, commensurate with the development of the welfare state in the late 1940s, she wrote two influential reports which established the curriculum for the first social work training courses. Implicit within her recommendations was the notion that research needed to be consistently undertaken into the effectiveness of practice, and that social work research should be an active component within academia (**Younghusband** 1947).

It is debateable if this early vision to explicitly link practice with research was ever achieved. Following the creation of professional social work most government reports have concentrated on the configuration and organisation of the profession but have been less enthusiastic regarding the relationship between research and practice. For example, the influential Seebohm Report (1968), which led to the creation of generic local authority social services departments, acknowledged the need for research but saw this as being no more than an audit of local needs and aspirations within the remit of community development as opposed to rigorous academic enquiry (Glasby 2005).

In more recent years, however, there has been a renewed emphasis placed on the relationship between research and practice, not least due to the need to improve the credibility of social work following a number of critical inquiries and the establishment of the three-year university-based social work degree. This renewed interest was made explicit in 2001 with the creation of the SCIE which has the following aims.

- to capture and co-produce knowledge about good practice. To carry out and commission research and work with other leading organisations to produce information and practical guidance about what works in social care;
- to communicate knowledge, evidence and innovation. To share our knowledge about what works in partnership with sector partners including improvement agencies, networks of providers, groups of people who use services, including children, young people, their families and carers, regulators and government departments.

(**www.scie.org.uk**)

As can be seen from these stated aims, an important strand of the work of SCIE is to produce, collate and disseminate knowledge that informs and improves practice. It could be suggested that for the first time in its relatively young history, social work has begun to fulfil the vision of Dame Younghusband.

Despite these attempts to embed research into social work practice the relationship has never been straightforward. In part this is due to a lack of consistent funding from government, a lack of time by frontline staff to be able to thoughtfully consider the findings of research and translate them into practice, and a measure of mistrust regarding the claims of research by practitioners.

Chapter Summary

In this chapter we used the typology devised by Pawson et al. (2003) as a framework to allow us to discuss the component parts of knowledge that contribute to social work. We adopted an uncomplicated approach which used the division between 'informal' and 'formal' knowledge provided by Pawson et al. (2003). First, in our discussion of informal types of knowledge we considered practitioner knowledge and noted concerns regarding its subjective and untestable nature. We also highlighted the fact that other allied disciplines with historically greater connections to science, such as medicine, were also beginning to appreciate the relevance of such insights. Using the model developed by Dreyfus and Dreyfus (1986) we then noted the way in which practitioner knowledge becomes increasingly important as professionals gain more confidence in their skills and experience in their role. We then sought to distinguish between service user and carer knowledge, arguing that both offer discrete perspectives which are complementary but distinct. A central argument was the need to acknowledge and use the subjective knowledge a service user or carer brings to the social work relationship. Often this knowledge is disregarded and seen as 'second best', much in the same way that practitioner knowledge can be devalued by those who would propound a more scientific, rational approach to practice.

We then briefly looked at more formal sources of knowledge – in particular, policy community knowledge and organisational knowledge – and offered some working examples for you to consider. Finally, we introduced you to some of the issues regarding research and suggested that a working relationship between research and practice has not always been achieved. We briefly traced the evolution of social work and suggested that the intention to incorporate research is systematically alluded to in policy but remains more elusive in practice.

In terms of critical thinking skills you were specifically invited to reflect (skill 7) on issues raised in the text on a number of occasions. Examples are given below.

- You reflected on the role of practitioner knowledge, service user knowledge and carer knowledge and reviewed the advantages and disadvantages of these more subjective types of knowledge.
- You were also asked to reflect on power differentials between academic researchers and service users/carers and to consider that a similar disparity exists between practitioners and service users.
- You also reflected on the fact that subjective knowledge is sometimes more applicable, more useful in its application than knowledge generated by formal research.

The other critical thinking skills you used involved

- a debate concerning the validity of subjective knowledge and how such forms of knowledge challenge traditional hierarchies of knowledge (skill 2);
- an evaluation of the different perspectives and ideas offered to the search for knowledge by service users and carers (skill 4).

This chapter has been introductory in nature and we will return to some of the themes in a more critical and in-depth way later in the book. The intention was to help you to understand and examine the different strands of knowledge that inform practice. In our next chapter, having set out the foundations of social work knowledge, we begin to critically explore the interface between knowledge and social work practice. In particular, we question the objectivity of knowledge and the ways in which practitioners use knowledge. Our debate has some way to travel yet and we hope that you enjoy the journey.

Further reading

Glasby, J. and Beresford, P. (2006) Who knows best? Evidence-Based Practice and the Service User Contribution. *Critical Social Policy, 26* (1): 268–84.

This paper explores and critiques the concept of 'evidence-based practice'. In particular, it challenges the concept of hierarchies of evidence and stresses the validity of professionals' practice wisdom and the lived experience of service users.

Branfield, F. and Beresford, P. (2006) *Making User Involvement Work: Supporting Service User Networking and Knowledge*. York: Joseph Rowntree Foundation.

Available for free download from **www.jrf.org.uk**, this research report explores the state of user networking and knowledge with the aim of ensuring that user knowledge becomes integrated in the evidence base of health and social care policy and practice.

Social Care Institute for Excellence (SCIE) **www.scie.org.uk**

The Social Care Institute for Excellence (SCIE) is an independent registered charity whose mission is to 'identify and spread knowledge about good practice to the large and diverse social care workforce and support the delivery of transformed, personalised social care services'. SCIE pull together knowledge from diverse sources through working with a broad range of people and organisations. Their work covers the breadth of social care, including services for adults, children and families; participation; human resource development; social work education; and e-learning.

Part Two

3 How does social work engage with knowledge?

Ian Mathews

Achieving a Social Work Degree

Exercises and content in this chapter will focus on

- skill 1 demonstrating understanding and application of theoretical ideas
- skill 2 comparing and contrasting different viewpoints and experiences
- skill 3 relating different views to underlying philosophies or ideologies
- skill 7 reflection

In addition its content is particularly relevant to the following Social Work Subject Benchmarks.

4.6 recognise and work with the powerful links between intrapersonal and interpersonal factors and the wider social, legal, economic, political and cultural context of people's lives
understand the impact of injustice, social inequalities and oppressive social relations
challenge constructively individual, institutional and structural discrimination

4.7 gain the ability to acquire and apply the habits of critical reflection, self evaluation and consultation, and make appropriate use of research in decision-making about practice and in the evaluation of outcomes

5.1.2 understand the complex relationships between public, social and political philosophies, policies and priorities and the organisation and practice of social work, including the contested nature of these

5.1.4 gain the ability to acquire and apply knowledge and critical appraisal of relevant social research and evaluation methodologies, and the evidence base for social work

Introduction

So far in this book we have introduced you to a number of themes relating to the knowledge that underpins and supports professional social work practice. In this chapter, however, we build on these initial ideas and begin to explore the practical application of knowledge in social work practice. For knowledge, however it is understood or classified, needs to serve a practical purpose otherwise there is a danger that it is conceived of as abstract and purely part of an academic debate.

We would argue, however, that in order for knowledge to be 'fit for purpose' it needs to be questioned by the practitioner. In this chapter we briefly discuss two processes which can assist the practitioner to analyse knowledge, namely reflective practice and supervision. While these vehicles are clearly of importance they are merely examples of ways in which knowledge can be assessed and verified. We argue that within and outside of these fora the practitioner needs to have a range of questions and principles with which to examine knowledge. Finally, in this chapter we raise some important considerations regarding the value base of social work and how we need to guard against an uncritical acceptance of knowledge without first questioning the basis of how that knowledge has been produced. There will also be opportunities for you to further develop your skills of analysis. For example, in this chapter you will come across a range of theoretical concepts (skill 1) with which you will need to engage. One way of doing this is to compare and contrast the different viewpoints and ideologies (skills 2 and 3) that underpin and inform these ideas. We spend some considerable time in this chapter considering reflection (skill 7) and it is our hope that you will reflectively engage with what we have written. This should not be a passive activity but one that critically analyses what you have read and the different thoughts and theories which have been introduced to you. It is permissible to disagree with what we have written. As we hope you will have discovered by now, knowledge is a difficult subject with which to grapple and part of that engagement involves producing your own ideas and knowledge.

The interrogation of knowledge

As a starting point for this chapter we want to encourage you to think about ways in which the knowledge that informs social work practice can be analysed or questioned.

Critical thinking exercise 3.1

Consider what strategies or tools the practitioner may be able to use to determine if the knowledge they use in their role is relevant, trustworthy and useable.

One obvious way in which this process may happen is through what is commonly termed 'reflective practice'. Reflective practice has become something of a 'buzzword' in social work in recent years and features in many of the standards that guide the profession. For example, it is a key aspiration within the National Occupational Standards (TOPSS 2002) and the Social Work Degree benchmarking statements (QAA 2008). It is not within the remit of this book to provide a comprehensive debate regarding 'reflective practice' as our primary focus is on evidence and knowledge. Nonetheless, a brief summary of some of the key ideas central to reflective practice will help us to understand the context in which it may support the active consideration of knowledge. As with many frequently used terms, reflective practice is open to critique and can refer to a number of intuitive and cognitive processes (Ixer 1999; Brookfield 2009).

Key idea 3.1: **The evolution of reflective practice**

It could be argued that the debate regarding professional reflection can be traced back to the 1980s and the work of American social scientist Donald Schön. **Schön** (1983) was instrumental in devising a twofold classification of how professionals acquire the skills and knowledge which are essential to their role. He describes the first approach as being 'technical-rational', where a situation always responds in the same way to the same set of actions. Consequently, a practitioner can learn the skills required to solve the problem through demonstration and modelling. **Parker** (2004) provides a good example of this approach when he refers to a junior surgeon who is taught by a more experienced colleague how to perform a minor operation. The skills are incrementally passed on via demonstration and the junior surgeon gains expertise by modelling his or her practice on that of the senior surgeon. **Schön** (1983) argues that this approach is workable as long as the problem is fixed and can be resolved by following an agreed set of actions. In social work we would argue, however, due to the fluidity and complexity of the presenting problem and the uniqueness of the context, this approach is often insufficient.

Schön's second approach is entitled 'reflection-in-action' and focuses on the use of tacit, intuitive knowledge and how this knowledge is refined by the professional during practice. As the name of this approach implies, the professional is required to actively critique and develop their knowledge base while simultaneously performing their duties. You may reflect that this process has connections to our discussion of 'practice wisdom' in Chapter 2 where we argued that knowledge gained and refined through experience forms an important component of social work practice.

In both of these approaches identified by **Schön** (1983) the worker essentially relies on pre-existing knowledge. Any reflection that occurs is limited and is more improvisation than a robust critical analysis of the worker's knowledge base. These facets are summarised and taken further by **Nathan** (2002: 66) in his discussion of the work of Schön.

A common experience of social workers is that they know much more than they can explicitly articulate. Theirs is a tacit knowledge. In his [Schön's] terms, their competency is formulated around a 'knowing in action' and/or a 'reflection in action'. In both forms of knowledge, the knowing or reflection is embedded in the action as revealed in the skilful execution of the task in hand without, characteristically, being able to make verbally explicit the theoretical or research base for that action.

You may have noted that **Nathan** (2002) includes reference to two further concepts. 'Knowing in action' refers to the ability of the practitioner to spontaneously implement action without necessarily having the ability to articulate the knowledge that underpins this action. 'Reflection in action' suggests a growing expertise which is able to combine and use knowledge gained through education, training, supervision and experience.

The control of knowledge

Schön's theoretical understanding has been critiqued and reworked on a number of occasions, but remains a helpful starting point. An interesting criticism of attempts to define the nuances and processes of reflective practice has been that reflection is sometimes seen as an end point in itself and that the importance of outcomes has been ignored (Ixer 1999). We would argue that reflection only serves a purpose if it generates an outcome, that of enabling the practitioner to use the process to make better decisions. This point is supported by **Ixer** (1999: 522–3)

> *Practitioners are seen as applying knowledge built up from their own experience which is 'tacit' and therefore difficult to access and discuss. Reflection aims to develop conscious control of knowledge in such circumstances, through a process of metacognition, so that professionals are able to self-analyse and learn to operate more effectively in demanding situations.*

If we analyse this statement we see that Ixer is suggesting that there is a sequential process that occurs in critical reflection. First, the practitioner is sufficiently experienced to have gained a range of useable knowledge which has become internalised or implicit. Second, the practitioner uses the process of reflection to make this knowledge explicit. By implication, the practitioner reviews and shapes knowledge until s/he develops 'conscious control' of it. Finally, the outcomes produced by this process are clear to see: an ability to analyse self and an increased effectiveness in practice.

We would, however, like to debate further the notion of a 'conscious control of knowledge'. Ixer (1999) suggests that this occurs 'through a process of metacognition'. To simplify, he is arguing that knowledge can be interrogated and controlled by the practitioner through the use of reason and self-awareness which leads to an understanding of how they think through problems.

Critical thinking exercise 3.2

Do you think that it is possible for a social worker to 'control' knowledge in the way implied by Ixer? Make a note of the ways in which this may happen and identify some of the difficulties that may make this process problematical.

We feel that it is debatable if a social worker can ever be fully in 'control' of the gamut of potential knowledge that they may be called on to deploy. If we also consider the level of complexity that a social worker is likely to encounter, it is unlikely that anyone will be able to instantly access every facet of knowledge that they will require. Clearly there is a requirement that social workers are knowledgeable within their field and should be able to offer insightful and informed input into any professional encounter. But equally a core skill of practice is the ability to seek advice from others who are more knowledgeable and to have the humility to acknowledge that no one knows everything all of the time.

It is helpful to note a further distinction in the process of critical reflection. In contrast to the arguments made by Ixer and Schön, Eraut (1995) suggests that the practitioner cannot reflect and act at the same time. He argues that on those occasions when a practitioner takes action in a situation demanding an immediate response it is likely that any reflection will be limited and passive in character. Under such circumstances, it is perhaps normal to be unable to describe the knowledge that underpins and guides action. In order to move beyond this reflective passivity, the worker needs to cognitively remove themselves from the situation in order to give themselves 'space' to reflect. This does not necessarily mean physical removal, but refers more to the space to think and consider. Conversely, Tate and Sills (2004) argue that the professional needs to be actively involved in a situation before they can begin the process of sifting and reviewing knowledge. In this paradigm, knowledge is seen as transformative and as a key component in the development of practice and of the personal and professional 'self'. This distinction is interesting as it brings into relief some of the difficulties we have when we consider how knowledge is processed and used in practice situations.

Finally, in our discussion regarding the 'control of knowledge' an interesting historical model is provided by progressive American philosopher John Dewey (1859–1952) who wrote extensively on the philosophy of education.

Dewey's model of problem solving

Dewey (1910) was primarily concerned with education and argued that children did not attend school as 'empty vessels' but came equipped with their own limited understandings and experiences of the world. It was subsequently the role of the teacher to use this knowledge as both a starting place and a continuing reference point for educational activity. Without wishing to force the analogy, it could be suggested that there is a connection here to Schön and some of the other writers we have considered in this chapter, who suggest that practitioners possess a starting point of intuitive knowledge which needs to be developed and refined by the rigours of practice and reflection.

As part of a wider debate about thought, action and knowledge, Dewey developed a five-stage model of problem solving.

The first stage provides a context for the process of knowledge interrogation. Dewey argues that the problem or issue to be confronted needs to be suitably complex and problematical in order to stimulate questioning and creative reflection. The idea that some solutions require a strong stimulus in order to be framed has been suggested on a number of occasions. For example, theorists of crisis intervention such as **O'Hagan** (1994) argue that service users who are undergoing rapid change and uncertainty are more amenable to the development of new solutions. While everyday social work practice may not routinely be crisis-ridden, it is possible to see that the task of making sense of a complex, fluid situation is sufficiently demanding to stimulate the questioning of knowledge.

In stages two and three, the problem solver begins to reflectively address the situation using imagination, hypothesis and metacognition which enables a tentative solution to be formulated. Dewey, however, argued that this potential solution needed to be tested and verified in action before it could be accepted as reliable knowledge. Consequently, any solution developed by reflection needs to be held in abeyance until the practitioner is able to verify its worth in practice.

In the final stages the solution is critically analysed through a process of rational deduction, and finally put into practice. Or, to use Dewey's phrase, it undergoes 'experimental corroboration'. The tentative explanation or solution is tested in the crucible of practice and ultimately provides new insights for the worker to use. This analysis is critical as it transforms and elevates tacit knowledge into a more explicit form of knowledge which can then become part of a deliberate thought process.

adapted from **Dewey** (1910), **Ixer** (1999), and **Westbrook** (1993)

A number of assumptions and commonalities underpin these different theoretical understandings. For example, there is a measure of agreement that practitioners find it difficult to articulate the knowledge that guides practice, and that much of this knowledge is intuitive in nature. Nonetheless, through a number of cognitive processes it is possible to gain at least a measure of control over this knowledge. Without wishing to overextrapolate, we may suggest that this skill comes with experience. The more experienced you are, the more able you are to recall and explicitly use knowledge in practice. Interestingly, this assertion contradicts the work of Dreyfus and Dreyfus (1986) whom we referred to in Chapter 2. They argue that one of the defining characteristics of the 'expert' practitioner is the ability to depart from established procedures and knowledge and to work in an increasingly intuitive way. There are some key differences, however, that we need to note. Tate and Sills (2004) and Ixer (1999), for example, broadly agree that this process of knowledge interrogation must occur during practice. Dewey (1910) and Eraut (1995) conversely suggest that the practitioner needs to be removed, at least cognitively if not physically, from the arena of practice if reflection is to be successful.

Finally, there is some agreement that this processing of knowledge involves the objective use of reason, intellect and cognition. The outcome of this struggle is that practitioners are able to articulate their knowledge base and more effectively operate in practice through the explicit incorporation of knowledge into practice.

Optional further study

The article by Graham **Ixer** (1999) was a landmark piece of writing which crystallised a number of ideas regarding the role of reflective practice in social work. Although now a little dated, it remains one of the foundational texts on the subject.

Key idea 3.2: **The use of supervision in the interrogation of knowledge**

Another process that can assist the social worker to test knowledge is the supervisory process. Supervision can occur in a number of different ways but is traditionally configured, at least in statutory social work, as a forum where a worker and supervisor (typically the line manager) meet together to discuss an amalgam of casework, organisational and managerial issues. There have been a number of criticisms of supervision, or rather the absence and limited quality of appropriate, timely and purposeful supervision, in recent years. For example, one of the significant criticisms raised by Lord Laming (2003) in his inquiry into the death of Victoria Climbié was the lack of rigour and oversight in professional supervision. It could be argued that due to the pressure placed on social care organisations to consistently meet defined performance targets and outcomes, supervision has become increasingly focused on meeting managerial objectives rather than promoting the professional growth and understanding of the worker (Wilson et al. 2008; Adams et al. 2009a).

This view is cogently expressed by **Noble and Irwin** (2009: 352) in their critique of how supervision has been eroded by economic and political factors:

We argue that the move to restrict supervision to monitoring worker performance at the expense of professional and intellectual growth is inhibiting the possibility of new and challenging practice dialogues and learning opportunities from emerging. Focusing on the tasks associated with management expectations and performance outcomes in supervision sessions closes off any opportunity to reflect on current issues and to develop strategic responses. It seems that engaging in reflection would seem 'too hard' or 'out of place' in this new economic climate.

Nonetheless, it is possible to see how the supervisory relationship can be a means of facilitating knowledge development. For example, Payne (1996) in his discussion of the role and purpose of supervision suggests a more balanced view.

Supervision

- has the primary function of protecting service users from harm or abuse. This may be achieved through updating the knowledge, skills or practice of the worker, ensuring that policies and protocols regarding safeguarding issues are followed, or by addressing inappropriate or dangerous practice;
- provides support for practitioners. This could be through the discussion of casework issues or difficulties, or through the provision of oversight/ recommendations/advice from the supervisor;
- is one method of ensuring that practitioners maintain and enhance their professional standards. This is clearly linked to the protection of service users and the provision of 'best organisational practice' but also refers to individual growth and development;
- ensures that workers understand what is required of them by the organisation and that tasks are delivered in a professional and competent manner.

While many of these functions appear to be process led and managerial in character, it is possible to see that the sharing and scrutiny of knowledge can be an integral facet of the supervisory relationship. For example, in order to promote 'best organisational practice', or to tease out the complexities of a 'difficult' case, both worker and manager need to be aware of departmental policy, national guidance, recent research findings and appropriate theory and be able to incorporate practitioner and service user knowledge. In other words, in order to be up to date and well informed, they need access to the range of knowledge we identified in our discussion of typologies in Chapter 2.

While the breadth of knowledge social workers need may be obvious, it is more pertinent to ask how that knowledge will be scrutinised within supervision. Noble (1999) suggests that supervision is an opportunity to articulate and then reflect upon a particular issue or approach. In her words it is an opportunity to make crucial links between 'thinking' and 'doing'. While this may sound simplistic, it makes a clear link with our previous thoughts on critical reflection. Supervision then is an opportunity to engage in critical thought and reflection with another person.

Optional further study

There have been a number of books written on the use of supervision within social work. For more experienced staff who are in employment the work of **Morrison** (2005) is a valuable resource. It is particularly helpful in reminding us that good supervision is as much for the benefits of service provision (and therefore the quality of service provided to users) as it is for staff. For students on training courses the book by **Lomax et al.** (2010) on 'placement survival' contains a range of advice and guidance on how to get the most out of supervision.

But we need to go further in our analysis. So far in this chapter we have identified two processes which enable us to question knowledge: critical reflection and supervision. There are clearly other ways and means of processing knowledge within professional practice, not least the sharing of views and perspectives with other colleagues, which can be especially valuable in a multidisciplinary setting. We now want to turn, however, to a discussion of how knowledge is analysed and evaluated. What questions need to be posed by the practitioner in order to ensure that the knowledge they use is reliable and trustworthy?

Critical thinking exercise 3.3

You may remember that in the introduction to this chapter we suggested that before knowledge can be seen to be 'fit for purpose' it needs to be questioned by the practitioner. Take some time to reflect on ways in which the knowledge used in practice can be analysed. What questions do you need to ask of a piece of knowledge in order to ensure that it is accurate, useful and valid?

In order to help us to begin to answer these questions we turn again to Pawson et al. (2003).

Research summary

Pawson et al. (2003: 37–40) suggest a number of ways in which knowledge should be evaluated and have developed the acronym 'TAPUPA' as a helpful way of remembering these principles.

Transparency

The process of knowledge generation should be open to outside scrutiny. For knowledge to meet this standard, it should make plain how it was generated, clarifying aims, objectives and all the steps of the subsequent argument, so giving readers access to a common understanding of the underlying reasoning.

Accuracy

All knowledge claims should be supported by and faithful to the events, experiences, informants and sources used in their production. For knowledge to meet this standard, it should demonstrate that all assertions, conclusions and recommendations are based on relevant and appropriate information.

Purposivity

The approaches and methodology used to gain knowledge should be appropriate to the task in hand, or 'fit for purpose'.

Utility

Knowledge should be appropriate to the decision setting in which it is intended to be used, and to the information need expressed by the seeker after knowledge. For knowledge to meet this standard it should be 'fit for use', providing answers that are as closely matched as possible to the question.

Propriety

Knowledge should be created and managed legally, ethically and with due care to all relevant stakeholders. For knowledge to meet this standard, it should present adequate evidence, appropriate to each point of contact, of the informed consent of relevant stakeholders. The release (or withholding) of information should also be subject to agreement.

Accessibility

Knowledge should be presented in a way that meets the needs of the knowledge seeker. To meet this standard, no potential user should be excluded because of the presentational style employed.

TAPUPA

Transparency – is it open to scrutiny?

Accuracy – is it well grounded?

Purposivity – is it fit for purpose?

Utility – is it fit for use?

Propriety – is it legal and ethical?

Accessibility – is it intelligible?

It is important to acknowledge that Pawson et al. (2003) did not intend this list to be used mechanistically as a tick box, but more as a starting point with which to begin the process of knowledge evaluation. As useful as these principles are, they cannot replace the judgement of the practitioner *in situ* and should not be seen as a comprehensive list of rules to follow. Nonetheless, as general principles they are useful. For example, they raise interesting questions about the different sources of knowledge we have considered. Is practitioner knowledge 'transparent'? Would it stand the test of being 'open to scrutiny' and challenge from other practitioners, or service users? Is all research used in social work accurate? In 2010 the well-respected medical journal *The Lancet* retracted an article it had published in 1998 by Dr Andrew Wakefield which had claimed a connection between the measles, mumps and rubella triple vaccination given to children with the development of autism and bowel disease. The General Medical Council stated that the researchers had acted dishonestly and irresponsibly and that their findings were invalid. While this example sits outside social work it is interesting to speculate how many social care research findings could be similarly flawed. You may remember from our discussion in Chapter 1 that we used the example of evidence provided by bodies such as the Eugenics Education Society, which was used to underpin the implementation of the Mental Deficiency Act 1913 with its emphasis on incarceration and segregation. Finally, in terms of 'accessibility' we could question how accessible and understandable many policy documents are which are produced as part of 'organisational knowledge'. On occasions, both practitioners, and more importantly service users, struggle to make sense of complex information produced by agencies.

Critical thinking exercise 3.4

The questions suggested by **Pawson et al.** (2003) provide a useful platform for the interrogation of knowledge, but clearly there are other approaches that could be adopted. Consider what other questions practitioners should ask when they are considering the reliability and validity of knowledge.

There are other important questions which need to be considered before knowledge can be deemed 'fit for purpose'. For example, we need to consider the effect that social constructions and cultural understandings have on the usefulness of knowledge. Sometimes, for example, there is a danger that we uncritically use research and knowledge which has been generated in very different cultural contexts. While such studies can be a real help to practice, we need to acknowledge the cultural uniqueness of the United Kingdom and the real differences that exist between Britain and even our closest cultural/geographical neighbours. As an example, research from North America which refers to social exclusion may have relevance to the United Kingdom, but equally we would need to acknowledge the differences that exist between the two countries in terms of demographics, race, cultural understandings, welfare benefit and insurance systems, employment opportunities and patterns, service provision, etc. before we could make an accurate judgement on the reliability of this knowledge.

Research summary

Clearly there is a balance that needs to be struck in the usage of knowledge. Social workers need to ensure that the knowledge they use in practice is applicable to their national and cultural setting. Equally, we need to guard against parochial and narrow-minded views that suggest that 'our' knowledge is best and therefore we can learn nothing from other contexts.

A casual study of the *British Journal of Social Work* for the latter part of 2010 revealed that the overwhelming majority of articles came from UK-based contributors. Additionally, there were a small number of contributions from Australia and single pieces of research from a diverse range of countries including Israel, South Africa and China. What was surprising was the lack of input from European academics. With the notable exception of Ireland and a single article from Norway there were no other European contributions. While it would be unfair to extrapolate too much from this observation it is at least interesting to note that social work activity and research from our nearest neighbours seems to receive such limited attention.

Optional further study

The report *Child Protection; Messages from Research* (**Department of Health 1995**) report contains an interesting section comparing the differences and commonalities between the results of research undertaken in the UK and the USA. It highlights differences in approach, legislation and cultural attitudes which further strengthen our stated position.

You may also have noted other issues that need to be considered. For example, in a fast-moving world knowledge quickly becomes dated. It is unlikely that a book or article or piece of practice wisdom from 20 years ago still remains relevant. Some elements of knowledge clearly 'stand the tests of time', but many are quickly superseded by new research, different ways of working and fresh insights.

Equally, you may have noted that a disproportionate number of books, journal articles, government/organisational policies and research studies are produced by middle-aged, middle-class, white men who occupy positions of power and authority. Without being overly simplistic, this reflects the structural realities of contemporary Britain where political life, management and academia are dominated by certain groups of people. This criticism is not new and has been voiced on a number of occasions, notably by **Thompson** (2006: 52) who, in his discussion of the pervasive role of sexism in society, argued that

> *One of the major implications for social work is the need to rethink radically the male dominated and masculine orientated basis of traditional social work theory.*

You may further reflect that social work is essentially a female profession while the knowledge that underpins its activities is often male generated. As social work borrows and acquires knowledge from a range of social science disciplines we need to be mindful of the gender bias that may underpin the production of this knowledge.

Critical thinking exercise 3.5

Critically consider those elements of sociology, psychology, social policy and other social sciences which provide knowledge that informs and guides social work practice. Make a list of the major theorists and identify how many are men and how many are women. If you find that there is an imbalance between male and female, consider why this is the case.

It is possible to compile a lengthy list of men who have contributed to the social sciences. But, as a brief example, all of the 'founding fathers' of sociology in the nineteenth century were male. Emile Durkheim (1858–1917) and Auguste Comte (1798–1857) were highly influential in developing positivism and were pivotal to the development of secular thinking regarding education and welfare provision. Karl Marx (1818–83) was the founder of communism and has contributed significantly to radical views within social work. Equally, Max Weber (1864–1920), the last of the founders of the discipline, offered insight into the bureaucracy and management that characterises large government organisations. In psychology, many of the principal thinkers who have shaped the discipline were men, for example, Sigmund Freud (1856–1939), the founder of psychoanalysis, whose work continues to influence thinking about childhood and sexual development. Erik Erikson (1902–94) and Jean Piaget (1896–1980), who followed in the footsteps of Freud, also remain highly influential in the understanding of childhood. Finally, the work of John Bowlby (1907–90) on attachment has been a mainstay of social work education for decades. Without overemphasising the point we could go on to name several dozen men who have made a significant contribution to the knowledge that underpins social work practice. When we turn our attention to women, however, it becomes less easy as academia has historically been almost the sole domain of men. This is not to undermine or diminish the contribution that women have made to the social sciences as there have been some notable female thinkers. They include Beatrice Webb (1858–1943), a social reformer who was instrumental in the founding of the London School of Economics, Rosa Luxemburg (1871–1919), a noted Marxist theorist, Simone de Beauvoir (1908–86), French feminist, existentialist and social theorist, Mary Ainsworth (1913–99), a North American psychologist whose pioneering work on mother/child separation informed the development of attachment theory, and Mary Wollstonecraft (1759–97), philosopher and feminist, whose writings subsequently informed the anarchist movement.

While these lists are neither comprehensive nor an accurate reflection of academic life there is a clear connection to oppression that we need to make. Historically women have had fewer opportunities to access education, gain employment in higher education, or to write for an academic audience. Consequently they have not had the same influence as men in the production of knowledge. As increasing numbers of women access jobs in academia, research and management it is possible that this imbalance may be rectified.

Equally, we could extrapolate away from this single issue and ask if other groups in society are fully represented in the production of knowledge. Although this is a difficult question to address, it is likely that we would find that there is a continuing underrepresentation of people who traditionally have found it difficult to access higher education, for example, people from a minority ethnic background, working-class people and disabled people. As we have already discussed in Chapter 2, in relation to service user knowledge, we may find that groups integral to our understanding of social work practice also have difficulty in getting their views and voices heard. Examples include children who have been in public care, people with learning difficulty or mental health problems.

Critical thinking exercise 3.6

What are the implications of this imbalance? Do you think that the possible exclusion of certain people and groups from research and academic life undermines the credibility of the knowledge and evidence used to underpin professional practice?

Let us first consider the implications for practice that arise from the gender imbalance that we have noted in our discussion. Thompson (2006) argues that social work takes place on the margins of what is considered to be 'normal' and what is seen as 'deviant'. It is the role of social work to police these borders and to control those individuals and groups who create problems for society through their 'deviance' (Singh and Cowden 2009). Thompson (2006) argues that this is not a neutral exercise as our understanding of what is 'normal' is gendered. For example, what we see as being a normal family is often based on patriarchal assumptions, while what we see as being 'good enough parenting' conversely often refers to the skills of the mother with little reference to the role of the father. In a real sense, these assumptions contribute to the reinforcement of gendered stereotypes as to what it means to be a family, a father and a mother. Knowledge has a key role to play in the creation and development of these gendered stereotypes. If theory, research and academic work is overwhelmingly undertaken by men it is reasonable to infer that often a male world view influences the knowledge produced and therefore used in practice.

The other imbalances we have noted should also concern us. Part of the criticality that we would encourage you to adopt in your approach to evidence or knowledge-based practice is an examination of 'where the writer comes from' – or, as part of this discussion, 'where they don't come from'. For example, we need to be aware of the political background or perspective of people who produce and disseminate knowledge that underpins social work practice. Sometimes, especially in terms of policies that derive from local or national government, this is clear to see, while on other occasions it is more difficult. Previously we noted the contribution to social science of Karl Marx and Rosa Luxemburg who adopt an overtly political standpoint in their writings. You may also note that later in this chapter we highlight the fact that Brookfield (2009) writes from a 'radical' perspective as a way of alerting you to his position. Other writers that have influenced social work thinking are equally open as to their political stance. One example is Charles Murray (1990) who gained prominence with his thesis regarding the rise of the 'underclass' in the 'sink estates' of the United States and Britain. As can be seen from the pejorative language that Murray employs he writes from a neo-liberal perspective and often contributes his views to conservative 'think tanks' and organisations.

We hope that you can see that analysing knowledge is a necessary prerequisite for the thoughtful practitioner and that it is not acceptable to uncritically view evidence which is presented to you. Knowledge and evidence is not neutral and, as we argued in Chapter 1, it cannot be regarded as being 'truth'. It can only be viewed through the prism of subjective interpretation and will always contain within it biases and perspectives which need to be acknowledged and critically examined.

Key idea 3.3: **The interrelationship of values and knowledge**

So far in this chapter we have suggested that the significance and validity of the knowledge that guides social work practice can be tested by a range of tools, including critical reflection and supervision, and that there are a number of questions or standards that can be deployed to measure the validity of knowledge. This questioning, however, is not sufficient in itself, as we would argue that knowledge in social work needs to be underpinned and informed by a sound value base. The most knowledgeable practitioner who has no awareness or understanding of the value base of social work will have limited foundations on which to base their practice or their use of knowledge. We also need to recognise that there is a two-way process in operation here, for values in turn are informed and strengthened by knowledge. For example, many social workers and students undertaking professional qualification will be familiar with the PCS (Personal Cultural Structural) model of discrimination outlined by Thompson (2006). In brief this is an attempt to analyse the different ways in which oppression embeds itself into the fabric of society and how it manifests itself in the lives of oppressed people. We could suggest that the more informed and knowledgeable a social worker is regarding such analyses the more robust their value base will be and consequently the better their practice.

These insights are supported by **Brookfield** (2009: 297) who, writing from a radical perspective, offers an interesting critique of what often passes for critical reflection, in which he argues that

> *I contend that reflection is not, by definition, critical. It is quite possible to practise reflectively while focussing solely on the nuts and bolts of process, and leaving unquestioned the criteria, power dynamics and wider structures that frame a field of practice. Critical reflection turns the spotlight onto issues of power and control.*

This comment is interesting as it returns us to our previous discussion regarding the use of reflection. For Brookfield (2009) is arguing that as part of the process of reflection the worker needs not only to interrogate knowledge but also to consider the wider context in which this knowledge is generated, disseminated and sustained. In his view, knowledge used in social work reflects the oppressive nature of capitalism and often serves to promulgate beliefs that sustain economic and political inequity. Again, you will note that this view coincides with our discussion regarding the lack of involvement in academic work of women and some minority groups. This could be seen as a consequence of capitalism which promotes the male/female division of labour and safeguards the privileges of those in positions of dominance.

Singh and Cowden (2009) expand on this argument further by suggesting that social work has undergone a process of 'de-intellectualisation' over recent decades. Successive governments have emphasised the more controlling aspects of the role which require the professional to provide a service that 'works' but do not attempt to explain (or address) the underlying issues of social exclusion, poverty and social injustice that have brought service users into the orbit of social work in the first place. They argue that social work has been reduced to little more than a technical process devoid of any intellectual activity or knowledge production which would raise questions about the basis of contemporary practice. Social work has been reduced by successive governments from being a progressive profession capable of challenging injustice and oppression to one that meets government performance targets, treats users as customers, and accepts restrictive financial budgets. Crucially, social workers are no longer encouraged to theorise, intellectually critique their role, or to use knowledge as a means of emancipation.

Using the analogy of a commercial transaction, **Singh and Cowden** (2009: 490) exemplify their argument thus:

When you go into a hardware shop to buy a light bulb, you don't want a fancy explanation of how light bulbs work, you want a light bulb that 'works'. By extension, social workers are not there to provide 'fancy' explanations of poverty, racism, homophobia or any form of social exclusion, they are there to provide the service; this is what the customer wants.

Implicit within their argument is the conviction that social workers need to fuse an analytical critique of knowledge with a value base that emphasises the search for social justice as a necessary antidote to the reductionism of government and the de-intellectualisation of the profession.

Both of these arguments raise a fundamental question which challenges the initial typology of knowledge and the TAPUPA acronym provided by Pawson et al. (2003). It could be argued that Pawson et al. are presenting a conformist view of social work knowledge. The typology of knowledge they suggest raises few concerns about the basis of that knowledge, while the quality standards they propose do not seem to include a radical questioning of the contextual framework of knowledge. There appears to be an underlying assumption that the foundations of knowledge are sound and that any problems that arise from social workers using knowledge stem from an inadequate grasp of that knowledge or the inability to relate knowledge to practice. While this synopsis of Pawson et al. (2003) may be a generalisation, it emphasises the contentious nature of the use of knowledge in social work and reminds us again of the importance of criticality.

Chapter Summary

In this chapter we started by briefly discussing two vehicles, reflection and supervision, which could be used as a means of testing the validity of knowledge. This discussion enabled us to move away from process to consider how knowledge is tested and raise the question, can a social worker ever be fully 'in control' of knowledge? Using the work of Schön (1983) and Ixer (1999) and others we discussed some of the ways in which social workers use cognition and reason to work with intuitive knowledge in practice.

We then reconsidered the work of Pawson et al. (2003) who suggest a number of principles which can be used to evaluate knowledge based on the acronym TAPUPA (which stands for **T**ransparency, **A**ccuracy, **P**urposivity, **U**tility, **P**ropriety, **A**ccessibility). Finally, we returned to a consistent theme, that of the explicit link between knowledge and values. When using knowledge we always need to use what Noble and Irwin (2009) call a 'critical lens'. That is, we must be mindful of how knowledge is produced and whose interests are implicitly or explicitly served by the subsequent use of that knowledge.

We hope that you have enjoyed this chapter as the critical thinking that has underpinned it forms the basis for an ongoing critique of knowledge. In terms of critical thinking skills you were specifically invited to

- demonstrate understanding and application of theoretical ideas in a debate concerning the processes that occur when a practitioner attempts to synthesise and produce knowledge in practice. You may recall that we used the work of several authors, for example Schön (1983), to explore intuitive knowledge and how practitioners sometimes find it difficult to articulate their knowledge base (skill 1);
- compare and contrast different viewpoints, philosophies and experiences, which you did by analysing the context of knowledge production. You considered how knowledge is often produced by certain sections of society and how we need to be aware of the cultural and political context of knowledge production (skills 2 and 3);
- Reflect on the role and purpose of reflective practice and supervision (skill 7).

In our next chapter we continue our debate regarding values, analyse the uniqueness of the knowledge base in social work and, importantly, begin to look at some of the limitations and failings of knowledge in professional practice.

Further reading

White, S., Fook, J. and Gardner, F. (eds) (2006) *Critical Reflection in Health and Social Care*. Berkshire: Open University Press.

This collection of edited chapters is written in four parts which consider the frameworks for understanding critical reflection, critical reflection for professional learning, research and education. Of particular interest in relation to your learning in this chapter is Chapter 10, 'Using critical reflection in research and evaluation', written by Fiona Gardner (pages 144–55). Within the chapter, Gardner considers the key principles for thinking about research and evaluation (page 146).

Brown, K. and Rutter, L. (2008) *Critical Thinking for Social Work* (2nd edition). Exeter: Learning Matters.

In this book, the authors consider notions of critical thinking, critical reflection and critical practice. Chapter 3 is titled 'Learning – applying new knowledge to practice' and reinforces many of the issues discussed within the current chapter of this book.

Knott, C. and Scragg, T. (eds) (2010) *Reflective Practice in Social Work*. (2nd edition) Exeter: Learning Matters.

As part of the series 'Transforming Social Work Practice' this book will further your understanding of how, following the title of Knott's Chapter 4, reflection in practice can act as a 'catalyst for change', through using supervision, colleagues and practice assessors to support and add depth as you reflect on and question the knowledge for practice.

4 What influences the evolution of social work knowledge?

Ian Mathews

Achieving a Social Work Degree

Exercises and content in this chapter will focus on

- skill 2 comparing and contrasting different viewpoints and experiences
- skill 4 evaluating different perspectives and ideas
- skill 6 synthesising arguments
- skill 8 reviewing, re-evaluating and reformulating your own views

In addition its content is particularly relevant to the following Social Work Subject Benchmarks.

4.7 think critically about the complex social, legal, economic, political and cultural contexts in which social work practice is located

5.1.2 the location of contemporary social work within historical, comparative and global perspectives, including European and international contexts

5.1.4 research-based concepts and critical explanations from social work theory and other disciplines that contribute to the knowledge base of social work, including their distinctive epistemological status and application to practice

Introduction

Throughout this book we have consistently challenged you to examine the veracity and validity of the knowledge base that underpins and guides social work practice. As you may have concluded, even reaching agreement on what constitutes knowledge and deciding what aspects of knowledge are essential to social work practice is a difficult task. You will recall from the work you did in Chapter 2 that there are a number of typologies and systems of classification that help tease out the various components of social work knowledge. Additionally, it is often assumed, not least in the curricula that guide social work education, that the traditional social sciences of sociology, psychology and social policy are among the building blocks of social work practice. To an extent we reinforced that perspective in Chapter 3 in our discussion of the principal theorists within the social sciences whose work informs social work practice.

There are, however, some who question the viability, or even the wisdom, of attempting to define the knowledge base of social work. For example, Payne (2001) argues that such is the increasing specialisation within social work that some elements of knowledge which are viewed as essential in one specialism are rarely, or never, used in another area. This thought may correspond with your practice setting, especially if you have experience in a specialist team, and is a point which we will revisit on a number of occasions in this chapter. Payne (2001) also suggests that what universities, practitioners or regulatory bodies may consider to be core knowledge is dependent on a range of biases and factors; not least who has the power to define what is considered to be essential knowledge and what is needed by the profession at that point in time. For example, in the 1980s in UK social work the concept of 'anti-oppressive practice' was of particularly relevance due to a range of contextual and political factors. While anti-oppressive practice in various guises remains a feature of social work it has been overtaken, or at least joined, by other contemporary theoretical emphases such as 'reflective practice' and 'globalisation'. In conclusion, Payne suggests that the knowledge which informs practice is not so much a base but more of a fluid, evolving process. Although Payne's thoughts are contentious they are also helpful as they remind us that social work is a dynamic profession that does not and cannot stand still.

With this notion of movement and evolution in mind, we take our debate forward by exploring a number of factors which we argue have stimulated change in the knowledge base of social work. As always we need to be guarded when we enter into such a debate as it is not possible to identify and analyse all of the pressures that move professional knowledge forward. You may well have your own ideas and perspectives, which could be very different to ours. Nonetheless, we have identified three factors which we feel are of particular relevance.

These are

- the growing influence of service user knowledge;
- the demands placed on social work knowledge by interprofessional settings and cultures;
- an examination of lessons that can be learnt from inquiries and reports produced as a response to high-profile failings in health and social care.

In terms of skill development, as so often in this book, we will be presenting a range of competing ideas and asking you to analyse them and to make your own judgement as to their validity. In particular in this chapter we suggest that skill 8, the ability to review, re-evaluate and reformulate your own views, is of importance as we ask you to analyse the drivers behind the evolution of the knowledge base of contemporary social work practice.

The use and abuse of service user knowledge

Throughout the course of this book we have consistently returned to a number of core themes and in this section we turn again to the issue of service user knowledge. In Chapter 2 we commented on the necessity of recognising and using the knowledge possessed by service users and carers. In that chapter we concentrated primarily on a personal definition of knowledge; that is, how a service user sees themselves and the knowledge they bring of their own situation and how it is vital to value this insight.

In this chapter we want to extend the debate further, but this time looking more at the ways in which knowledge produced by service users (and service user-led organisations) has shaped, and continues to shape, the professional task. In order to contextualise our debate we need to briefly revisit the origins and underlying principals of contemporary social work.

Research summary

The evolution of professional social work

Horner (2009), in his historical overview of social work, identifies a number of key nineteenth-century influences which moulded the evolution of social work. For example:

- the development of voluntary organisations, many of them created by faith groups, dedicated to 'saving' the orphan, 'rescuing' the prostitute and 'reforming' the drunkard. The positive contribution of voluntary organisations in the nineteenth century, especially in the support they provided to the dispossessed, urban poor has been well documented, although their questionable moral basis and emphasis on the 'deserving poor' needs to be acknowledged (**Mathews** 2009);
- the call by left-wing groups, notably 'the Fabians', led by reformers such as Beatrice and Sidney Webb, for the state to intervene in areas such as education, housing and employment. While this was essentially a progressive programme, the expectation was that the state would lead people out of poverty through the application of social policy. Nonetheless, the Fabians also recommended that state intervention should cure the work-shy and that detention colonies would be needed for the especially idle;
- the development of an 'enforcing role' by the state via legislation: for example, the development of compulsory elementary education for children and the increasing incarceration of the troublesome and the feeble-minded via the burgeoning institutional sector, which was briefly explored in Chapter 2.

It could be argued that these themes of rescuing the needy, the provision of universal services by the state, and an emphasis on social control have influenced the evolution of social work to the present day. While this is a simplistic and subjective argument, a recurrent theme is that of the state, or the social worker, 'doing things to' the recipient. There is no sense of partnership or mutuality – the state identifies the problem, often sites it within the individual, sets the agenda, and decides what will be done.

Coupled with this historical legacy, there has also been an increasing emphasis on the development of professionalism and expertise within social work, confirmed by the creation of a professional body, a degree qualification with a prescribed curriculum and a legally protected status. Although it could be argued that these reforms were long overdue, a by-product of this process has been a widening of the gap between the experience and knowledge of the service user and the power of the professional. Adopting an historical analysis, **Beresford and Croft** (2001: 300) argue that throughout its evolution

> *. . . social work has been an increasingly professionalised top down activity, whose main recipients have been largely marginal to its construction.*

This marginalisation has taken many forms, but for our purposes it is interesting to note how service user knowledge has been either disregarded or used to justify the existence of social work and how this is changing.

Key idea 4.1: **Service user knowledge and the construction of social work**

Beresford and Croft (2001: 300) argue that service user knowledge and experience, often in the form of case papers, reports and studies, has always been used *to legitimise, rationalise and promote social work*. Initially, when professional social work was in its infancy, these understandings were used as a basis for allocating and receiving funding. In more contemporary times, service user feedback and insights have been used more systematically as a means of bolstering the construction of academic theory/ research and the development of managerial rationales in practice. These processes have often failed to acknowledge the input of service user knowledge and have been explicitly based on the interpretation of that knowledge by the professional, as opposed to the user. In other words, those who organise, manage and deliver social work have used service user knowledge for their own purposes and not always for the benefit of users. Beresford and Croft, however, argue that in more recent years there has been a growing recognition of the contribution of service user knowledge to the construction of social work.

Critical thinking exercise 4.1

Beresford and Croft (2001) suggest that there has been a positive change in the way that service user-produced research/knowledge is viewed by the social work profession. Do you think that there is any evidence to support this view?

We would agree that there has been an increase in the quantity and quality of research and publication undertaken by users and service user-led organisations. This is particularly true in relation to mental health where organisations such as the 'Social Perspectives Network' (**www.spn.org.uk**) and the 'Hearing Voices Network' (**www.hearing-voices.org**) actively promote the publication of knowledge derived from personal experience.

Second, service user knowledge and experience is increasingly valued in education and training. While service user contributions may still be piecemeal in some areas, there is a growing acknowledgement that user-led teaching and research makes a significant difference to the educational experience.

Third, service users have been using their knowledge of services, and what it is like to be a receiver of services, to set standards within service provision. To an extent this has been fuelled by the consumerist climate that has developed in recent decades, which seeks to place the purchaser, or recipient of services, centre stage. Encouraged by legislation, such as the NHS and Community Care Act 1990, which explicitly emphasises the duty of the local authority to consult with stakeholders both individually and collectively, service users have taken an active role in evaluation and the quality control of services. As Warren (2007) indicates, there has been a plethora of policy and legislation in recent years which has stimulated the active involvement of service users and carers in all aspects of provision. Additionally, a feature of the purchaser–provider split, introduced by the drive towards care in the community and more individualised care packages, is that services themselves have been increasingly provided by service user-led organisations. This in turn has helped to develop a productive cycle where service user knowledge is increased and is then directly used to inform service delivery. You may reflect that this view is supported by Beresford and Croft (2001) who argue that there has been a qualitative evolution in the nature of service user involvement in knowledge production. Historically, service user voices were largely ignored, followed by a period where personal accounts were valued, leading to the contemporary position where service users and service user-led organisations are increasingly encouraged to take part in knowledge production.

You may be familiar with various 'models of participation', often depicted as ladders, which indicate how involved service users are in service delivery or organisational development. For example, **Arnstein** (1969) outlines eight stages of potential participation.

1 *Manipulation* and
2 *Therapy*. Both of these stages exclude the service user from any form of participation. The aims of any public involvement are to benefit the organisation and to educate the participants. Any plan or proposition espoused by the organisation is deemed to be non-negotiable.

3 *Informing.* Often little more than a one-way flow of information from the organisation to the citizen with no mechanism for challenge or meaningful feedback.
4 *Consultation.* Sometimes regarded as the first stage of participation but often tokenistic in nature.
5 *Placation.* Users or citizens are permitted to offer advice or suggest ideas but the power to make decisions remains with the organisation.
6 *Partnership.* Power is increasingly and incrementally redistributed through negotiation between citizens and power holders. Planning and decision-making responsibilities are shared through fora such as joint committees.
7 *Delegated power.* Service users are able to exercise real power and tangible influence. Powers delegated from the appropriate authority enables them to make decisions and to be accountable for them.
8 *Citizen control.* Service users take responsibility for planning, policymaking and managing a programme.

adapted from **Arnstein** (1969)

The work of Arnstein remains significant as being a foundational text in the participation of citizens in decision-making fora. A number of theorists have taken forward Arnstein's basic premise and developed other linear type processes which conceptualise service user involvement. For example, Hart (1992) has devised a ladder which describes the participation of children. His ladder is similar to Arnstein's and traces an evolution from non-participation through to projects which are initiated and controlled by children and young people. It may be possible to see from our discussion that there has been at least some movement in the way that service user knowledge is incorporated into social work, akin to the progression outlined by Arnstein and others. It would, however, be unwise to overly extrapolate or emphasise this evolution as there are many 'rungs of the ladder' yet to climb.

In order to explore how the construction of social work has been transformed by service user knowledge, we now want to explore two specific examples: first, by way of a case study, the evolution of the 'social model'; and second, a discussion of personalisation.

The service user contribution to knowledge: the social model

Many of you will be familiar with the idea of models and theoretical frameworks, which attempt to explain events or situations, for example, models of child development or mental illness. Models offer a general theoretical understanding of situations and are often open to interpretation and critique. Nonetheless, they are helpful as a shorthand way of understanding complex phenomena. With these limitations in mind, we now want to explore a model developed by and for service users which has driven forward social work practice.

CASE STUDY

The social model of disability

The social model of disability can be seen as a derivative of the Civil Rights movement in 1960s America, which primarily sought the emancipation of Black people and other groups of people oppressed by structural factors within society. In the early 1970s a group of physically disabled service users/activists formed the 'Union of the Physically Impaired against Segregation'. This group, initially using their own experiences and a sociological understanding of society as a baseline, argued that it was not so much their physical impairment which disabled them but the way in which society systematically isolated and excluded them (**Oliver** 1996). They further argued that traditional views of disabled people portrayed them as being passive recipients of services and benefits who required 'special' schools, workshops, day centres and training centres where they could be cosseted and managed far removed from 'normal' society.

In contrast to this disablist view, the social model of disability moves the focus away from individual inability and sites the problem as the way in which impaired people are excluded from mainstream society by inaccessible work environments, poor transport systems, discriminatory and inadequate health and social care provision, and consistently negative representations in the media (**Cunningham and Cunningham** 2009). As can be seen from the following list, theorists who have contributed to the model suggest that there are at least three types of barriers that disabled people have to contend with, including:

- *social-structural barriers* – social and political structures which limit the lives of people with impairments, for example, educational, health care and social care systems;
- *attitudinal barriers* – the inherent prejudice of individuals and cultures which view and portray impaired people as 'crippled' or 'work-shy' or as requiring care or pity;
- *environmental barriers* – the built environment and physical surroundings which are frequently inaccessible and hostile to disabled people.

An explicit understanding within the model is that there is a difference between 'impairment' and 'disability'. Impairment refers to the lack of a limb or a bodily function, while disability reflects the disadvantage or restriction of activity caused by the oppressive and exclusionary actions of society (**Oliver** 1996).

This pivotal distinction is of importance and has contributed to social work knowledge and practice in a number of ways. For example, it could be argued that it is one of the forerunners of anti-oppressive practice, which seeks to make an explicit connection between the impoverishment of individual lives and the oppressive social causes of these limitations (Thompson 2006). In a wider sense, it has contributed to a progressive perspective within contemporary practice, which does not seek to pathologise the individual for their limitations or failings, but prefers a more holistic approach that considers the social, cultural and political context in which the person lives. Again we remind you of the PCS model devised by Thompson (2006) as a tool of analysis. An even more explicit interpretation of this approach is apparent in what we might term 'radical social work', an understanding of social work that seeks to understand and interpret the actions of individuals, and the role of the practitioner, within the context of an oppressive capitalist system (Ferguson and Woodward 2009; Harris 2003). It has been argued that radical ways of working tend to ebb and flow in social work (Horner 2009), but there is at least a sense in more recent years that social workers are seeking to change 'the social system and not the individuals who receive, through no fault of their own, the negative results of social arrangements' (**Mulally** 1993: 124). It would be overly simplistic to suggest that the social model has been the sole driver of contemporary radical viewpoints but we hope that you can see that there are at least interconnections and commonalities between the approach and some ways of working.

Equally, the underpinning understandings of the social model have been used to theorise away from physical disability to consider other aspects of life. For example, there is a growing use of a social model of risk (Stalker 2003), while many contemporary analyses of mental illness are based on the premises of the social model (Gould 2010).

While it would be an uncritical analysis which suggested that the social model alone has created these paradigm shifts, we maintain that it is a significant piece of service user knowledge which has assisted the evolution of social work knowledge and has impacted positively on practice.

If the social model of disability can be seen as the 'philosophical basis for the disabled people's movement' (**Beresford and Croft** 2001: 304) it can also be viewed as a contributor to a policy development which has the potential to profoundly change the lives of many people: the personalisation agenda.

Personalisation: service user knowledge in action

Personalisation means thinking about public services and social care and support in an entirely different way: starting with the person rather than the service. It requires the transformation of adult social care. ”

Jones, cited in **Carr** (2010: v)

As can be seen from this visionary statement in the opening paragraphs of the SCIE's *Personalisation: A Rough Guide* (Carr 2010), the way that services are organised and delivered to adults, and potentially children, is undergoing a seismic change.

Personalisation

It is beyond the scope of this book to offer a comprehensive summary of such a complex and evolving piece of social policy, but using the **SCIE** (Carr 2010) guide as a basis you may find the following key points helpful:

The underpinning philosophy of Personalisation views the service user as someone with strengths, preferences and aspirations. This stands in contrast to traditional methods of service delivery where the person often had to fit in with organisational schedules, limitations and barriers outside of their control. The person is central to the process and is given as much choice and control over their care plan as possible. Personalisation interlinks with policies designed to combat social exclusion as there is an expectation that people will be able to access universal services such as transport, leisure and education, housing, health and opportunities for employment, regardless of age or disability.

There are a number of themes within personalisation:

Self-directed assessment a simplified assessment process that is led, as far as possible, by the person in partnership with the social care professional focusing on the outcomes the person wants to achieve. Assessment takes account of the individual's whole situation and the needs of carers, family members and others who provide informal support.

Personal budgets sometimes referred to as 'individual budgets'. In December 2007, *Putting people first* (HM Government 2007) proposed that all social care users should have access to a personal budget. Within parameters, the person has the freedom to purchase services of their own choosing to meet their assessed care needs. These services can be purchased from a range of providers such as:

- statutory social care services;
- the private sector;
- the voluntary or third sector;
- user-led organisations;
- community groups;
- neighbours, family and friends.

Access to their own budget frees users from having to use traditional services, such as local authority day care services, or being forced to 'fit in' with the restrictions of centrally organised services. Currently such payments are designed to address social care needs, but there is a growing debate as to how the NHS might respond to demands for 'personal health budgets' for patients with long-term conditions or mental health problems.

abridged from **Carr** (2010: 1–11)

It could be argued that the drift towards Personalisation has been evident within social care for some time. For example, Direct Payments have been a feature of care provision for some service user groups, notably people with physical disabilities, for a number of years. This move towards a more empowering way of assessing need and enabling users to purchase services of their choosing may be seen as a practical outcome of the social model of disability.

We would also argue that Personalisation has affected perceptions regarding how different types of knowledge are valued. In past chapters we have alluded to the idea that some types of knowledge are 'better' or more rigorous than others. For example, in Chapter 1 we stated that scientific knowledge generated by objective enquiry was deemed to be more reliable and useful than other forms of knowledge. Within this tendency to compose hierarchies of knowledge, professional knowledge based on expertise is viewed as being better than that of service users based on lived experience. Evaluations of Personalisation, however, indicate that at least some users feel that their knowledge is becoming more recognised. For example, one service user speaking of individual budgets said:

> *It was a way of me being in charge. I didn't feel like . . . Social Services was telling me what I should do, what they thought was best for me, I was able to say what I thought was best for me . . . they're [Social Services] beginning to realise that the users are the experts, they're people with the impairments who live with them every day . . .*
>
> **Rabiee et al.** (2009: 920)

An integral part of this re-evaluation of the value of service user knowledge is the way in which self-directed assessment relies on the view of the user or carer. This stands in contrast to previous ways of working which seemed to emphasise the power of the professional.

> *. . . in the previous assessments . . . we never actually really saw the paperwork, the social worker did it . . . It was a relatively short interview, they went away, they filled the paper in, they did all the paperwork and everything else and the [number of] hours came out of it ... no time did they [the professionals] come back to us and say 'we have done this piece of work, do you agree with this piece of work, do you need to change it?'*
>
> **Rabiee et al.** (2009: 921)

Critical thinking exercise 4.2

Reflect on what you have read concerning the connections between the social model and personalisation. Do you think it is valid to see personalisation as 'service user knowledge in action'?

Interprofessional working and its impact on knowledge

The second factor we want to analyse as a potential driver in the evolution of social work knowledge is that of interprofessional working. Over recent decades there has been an increasing emphasis on the desirability and need for practitioners to pool their knowledge and expertise in order to enhance the delivery of health and social care. To an extent this has been stimulated by successive government policies designed to enforce partnership working across agencies. For example, in adult care services one of the stated aims of the NHS and Community Care Act 1990 was to demolish the so called 'Berlin wall' – rigid barriers and ways of working that existed between the NHS and local authority social care services. In Children's Services, the Green Paper *Every Child Matters* (HMSO 2003) and the resultant Children Act 2004 (DCSF 2004) explicitly acknowledged that greater interprofessional and multi-agency work was necessary if the protection of vulnerable children was to be improved. Consequently, it is now common for social workers to be deployed in, or employed by, a range of organisations including health authorities, the private/independent sector or voluntary agencies. Equally, it is commonplace for non social care professionals such as nurses, occupational therapists or physiotherapists to be employed by statutory social care providers. In some teams, particularly in fully integrated services such as mental health or learning difficulty, it is not unusual for a social worker to be line-managed by someone from a health background and vice versa.

Optional further study

The work of **Bogg** (2008) provides a comprehensive discussion of some of the challenges and opportunities for social care workers within integrated mental health services. Chapter 9 is particularly helpful as it poses the question, where do service users fit in to new ways of working?

For workers providing leadership and management in more general integrated services the compilation by **McKimm and Phillips** (2009) addresses a range of issues including a thoughtful account of the role of spirituality (Chapter 6) by **Bernard Moss.**

This move towards fusion, collaboration and the sharing of interprofessional expertise raises a number of interesting questions about the impact this transition has had on social work knowledge. Equally, it poses the question, what impact has social work knowledge had on other professions? Could it be argued that this synergy has led to the development of new forms of knowledge that are unique to partnership working? In order to begin addressing these questions we want you to consider a particular practice scenario.

Critical thinking exercise 4.3

You may have noticed that we have introduced the term 'multidisciplinary' into our discussion. While there may be nuances and distinctions that divide the terms 'multidisciplinary' and 'interprofessional' we want you to view them pragmatically as referring to the same situation where professionals from several backgrounds work together.

Imagine that you are attending a child protection case conference that includes the following professionals:

- social worker;
- general practitioner;
- health visitor;
- educational psychologist;
- nursery school teacher;
- nursery school nurse;
- police officer;
- Sure Start representative.

What differences and commonalities can you identify in the knowledge that each professional will bring to the discussion?

Commonsensically we may suggest that there are some obvious differences. The meeting will rely on those professionals from a health/medical background to contribute specialist knowledge concerning the child's development and expertise regarding any injuries or illnesses. Colleagues from an educational background will need to contribute knowledge about the child's educational attainments and difficulties, while the police will be best placed to offer advice regarding possible criminal charges and court proceedings.

Equally, there will be many commonalities. All present should be able to use their knowledge of the child, its family and the social context to build a picture of the difficulties and inform outcomes or recommendations. Often this will involve an amalgam of sometimes more general information including knowledge of the family's history, an understanding of the local social and cultural environment, the current context of the family and areas of particular strength.

Research summary

Brandon, et al. (2005: 164) provide a positive example of how the pooling of interprofessional knowledge was instrumental in protecting a vulnerable child. In their research they encountered an incident where a midwife and health visitor had concerns over a child with a seemingly minor injury. Based on their knowledge of the past history of the family, and informed by information held by Children's Services and other health colleagues, further investigations were undertaken which revealed extensive injuries and action was taken to protect the child. Working collaboratively and sharing knowledge across health and social care services enabled this child to be appropriately protected and stands as a good example of interprofessional working.

Payne (2001: 135) suggests that a helpful way of considering the fusion of interprofessional knowledge is to see it as 'interdependent and interlocking'. He argues that there is a tendency for professional groups in health and social care to almost compete for dominion over an area of knowledge. Consequently, as professions compete for control of an area of expertise, over time their knowledge bases tend to merge. You may recall our case study in Chapter 1, concerning the rise to power of psychiatry where medicine successfully competed with the church and superstitious understandings of mental illness for the right to claim ownership of that area of knowledge. Payne (2001) argues that there exists a fluid mix of professions, or even groups within professions, whose knowledge overlaps and interacts and that it can be difficult for any group to claim that their profession has a unique knowledge base.

This argument is developed further by **Lymbery and Millward** (2009: 173), who suggest that the knowledge, skills and values of practice are 'common across numerous similar occupations' and that the real gift of social work to interprofessional working is its emphasis on the centrality of the service user. Furthermore, they suggest that social workers should embrace the inherent contradictions and differences within interprofessional working as the value base of the profession emphasises the acceptance of diversity and acknowledges the strength that different outlooks and knowledge can bring. These remarks are interesting as they again remind us of the connection between values and the use of knowledge which we discussed in Chapter 3.

Interprofessional working and the creation of new knowledge

While there is an argument that allied professions may possess the same knowledge base, it could also be suggested that new forms of knowledge are evolving as a result of the tensions caused by the interlocking and interdependence of professional knowledge described by Payne (2001). Earlier in this chapter we considered the social model and described it as an example of how service user knowledge has contributed to the evolution of social care. We want to briefly revisit this example, but this time to analyse how the tension between the social model and the medical model has led to the development of a new understanding.

The recovery model of mental health

Bogg (2008), in her discussion of the integration of health and social care professions in mental health services, argues that traditionally social care staff have espoused a social model understanding of mental distress with a corresponding emphasis on structural issues. On the other hand, health professionals have adopted a medical model approach which views mental distress as being an illness of the individual caused by chemical imbalance or faulty genes which can be treated and 'cured' (**Gould** 2010; **Golightley** 2009). Both of these ways of viewing mental illness have their place and both are supported by a research and an evidence base. **Bogg** (2008), however, argues that the conflict between these views has led to a search for a new, more inclusive understanding of mental illness.

The recovery model is a contested concept, but places an emphasis on the user's lived experience and states that recovery from mental illness is possible in 'whatever form this takes for the individual' (**Bogg** 2008: 47). While it relies heavily on psychosocial understandings, it does not dismiss the efficacy of medical intervention as long as this actively contributes to the recovery of the person. For our purposes, it is not necessary to go into detail about the construct of the model, as the process of how this new theory/knowledge evolved is of greater importance.

Bogg (2008) argues that the different professional groups and service users have been seeking a rapprochement to the inherent conflict between the medical and social models since the 1970s. Dissatisfaction with medical solutions and a desire to improve the experience of mental health service users led to the combining of biological, social and psychological perspectives and the knowledge that underpins them. This has ultimately led to the evolution of the recovery model in the 1990s.

Bogg (2008: 48) further suggests that

> *The inclusive nature of recovery has provided an opportunity for the disciplines to work in partnership, as it places equal value upon social, psychological and medical input. Each has something to contribute to the individual experience of mental health and mental illness.*

Without wishing to overemphasise the point, it could be argued that increased integration and interprofessional working in mental health, and the evident tensions produced by different outlooks, has led to an evolution in knowledge and practice. This new mutual knowledge has led to easier interprofessional relationships as there is shared ground as opposed to conflict. Moreover, **Bogg** suggests that the acceptance of recovery as a concept and the publication of clinical guidelines which incorporate the perspective by a range of health and social care bodies continues to add to this evolution. The process of amending and making knowledge fit for interprofessional practice is ongoing.

Finally, in this section we would like to invite you to consider your own experience.

Critical thinking exercise 4.4

Think about your own experience of interprofessional working. Can you identify any developments in thinking or knowledge which are the result of sharing expertise?

In some ways this is a difficult task. You may be able to identify new ways of working or new protocols or even more generally 'things that you do differently' as a result of sharing office space or casework with other professionals. Clearly, knowledge is important to these changes as evidence and understanding should underpin all change; although sometimes this is difficult to identify. Equally, you may be able to see how your value base has been stretched or challenged, or the influence you have had on other professionals in the way that they work. What we would encourage you to consider is that knowledge can never be static and that sometimes the challenge of having to consider diverse perspectives is helpful in clarifying both what we already know, and what we wished we knew!

The limitations of knowledge

The third and final factor we want to consider is the evidence produced by inquiries into failings in the health and social care systems; in particular, those elements which highlight weaknesses or gaps in knowledge.

Inquiry reports, such as those produced following the deaths of Victoria Climbié (Laming 2003) and Baby Peter Connelly (Laming 2009), are always distressing to read and often seem to contain the same familiar messages for practice. For example, Stanley and Manthorpe (2001) in their analysis of inquiry reports into cases involving mental health service users in the 1990s suggest that failings around poor communication, inadequate risk assessment and the management of workers involved in complex cases were common to many. Moving beyond these similarities we want to use the work of Stanley and Manthorpe (2001) as a starting point for a discussion of how inquiries can be helpful in identifying gaps in knowledge or areas of practice where social workers need to access specialist advice and guidance.

First, they allude to the role of alcohol identified in a number of mental health inquiries. For example, in the inquiry into the care of Anthony Smith (Wood et al. 1996), a young mentally ill man who stabbed his mother and stepbrother, it was noted that one of the reasons why he refused to take medication to control his psychotic symptoms was that it interfered with his enjoyment of alcohol. This will not come as a surprise to workers in mental health services where such situations are not uncommon. What is less recognised is the role that alcohol (and drug misuse) plays in violent crimes committed by people who have a diagnosis of mental ill health. While we need to be careful not to make simplistic connections regarding substance misuse and mental illness there is evidence that substance misuse is a factor in some high-profile cases where people have been assaulted or killed. For example, **Ward and Applin** (1998: 3) in their study of 17 homicide inquiry reports involving mentally ill people throughout the 1990s found that substance misuse was a significant feature in 14 cases. They argue that 'in 53% of cases alcohol or drug misuse could be . . . the major cause of homicide' (1998: 3). According to their report it would appear that these connections are often ignored or missed by workers who seem to be ignorant of the effects of substance misuse. Interestingly, despite the demonstrated connection, many of the subsequent inquiry reports make no recommendation regarding substance misuse.

We have consistently argued throughout this book that social workers need to possess a range of both specialist and general knowledge in order to be effective and efficient in their work. Often the breadth of knowledge required is underestimated and the increasing separation of different specialisms in practice is not always conducive to the acquisition of generic knowledge. Of course, it cannot be expected that every social worker will know everything there is to know about social work practice. You may recall that this is the thrust of the argument espoused by Payne (2001) with which we started this chapter. Nonetheless, it is concerning that on occasions when a gap in knowledge is identified there is no attempt to refer to colleagues who do possess this more specialist knowledge.

A further example is provided by Brandon et al. (2005) in their study of 20 serious case reviews involving death or significant harm to children in Wales. They argue that sometimes social workers failed to appreciate the need to access specialist knowledge in the assessment of parental ability. In particular, social workers failed to appropriately refer on learning disabled or mentally ill parents for specialist assessment. Consequently, this knowledge was not available to them when making profound decisions about capacity, risk and vulnerability. They also identified that gaps in knowledge had limited the ability of social workers to protect children and to make coherent case plans. For example, in a remark that echoes comments deriving from inquiries into mental health cases, they suggest that some workers were unrealistic in their view of parental substance misuse and how this could be treated. In particular, alcohol and drug misuse was viewed as being a lifestyle choice which could be curbed by abstinence as opposed to an addiction which required treatment.

To return to Stanley and Manthorpe (2001), they highlight another issue: two cases where there was considerable misunderstanding between mental health services and childcare teams. In the *Report into the Personality Disorder Unit, Ashworth Special Hospital* (Fallon et al. 1999) hospital social workers were criticised for their ignorance of child protection issues after allowing a sex offender to have unsupervised access to a child. Conversely, in the inquiry into the care of Darren Carr (Richardson et al. 1997), who set fire to a house killing three people, the inquiry team criticised child protection services for their lack of action and their poor understanding of mental health services.

This compartmentalisation of knowledge and the lack of understanding of workers beyond their area of specialism is alluded to by Lord Laming (2009) in his report into the death of Peter Connelly. In the report the inquiry team refer to concerns expressed over the missed connections between substance misuse, mental health, domestic violence and child protection issues which are pertinent to all areas of social work and, of course, relevant to the death of Peter Connelly. According to Lord **Laming** (2009: 38).

> “*It is estimated at least 200,000 children live in households where there is a known high risk case of domestic abuse and violence, with very many more affected at some point in time. Approximately 450,000 parents are estimated to have mental health problems; an estimated 250,000–350,000 children have parents who are problematic drug users, and around 1.3 million children live with parents who are thought to misuse alcohol. In this context, it is vital that professional staff working with adults are trained to identify and assess the needs of, and risk of harm to, children and young people.*”

It is noteworthy that the inquiry felt it necessary to add the final sentence. Presumably, this is because it was felt that adult care workers were ill equipped to assess the needs of children and did not possess the necessary skills or knowledge to appropriately protect them. It is also interesting as Laming's comments highlight the sheer complexity of the situations in which health and social care staff are routinely expected to work.

> The comments made by the Laming Inquiry regarding connections between multiple social issues and child protection are not new. The Department of Health report *Child Protection; messages from research* (1995) highlighted the high incidence of pre-existing offending behaviour, the lack of employment, limited educational achievements of parents and the influence of substance misuse in abusive families. Although this report is now dated, it unfortunately illustrates the continuing nature of issues within child protection.

These comments highlight the potential dangers of the increasing divisions within social work which rigidly seeks to separate work with children from work with adults from work with people with mental health problems and so on. We do, however, need to be balanced in our remarks and acknowledge that specialisation has been helpful in moving forward practice and providing service users with a more comprehensive, tailored service. What social workers need to remember is that there is a plethora of knowledge outside of their own specialist area which sometimes we need to be accessed. The recognition of the limitations of our own knowledge can be turned into a strength if it leads to greater collaboration, better communication between areas of practice and, of course, an improved social work service.

Chapter Summary

In this chapter we have identified three factors which have had an impact on social work knowledge. They are only examples of a range of factors and we do not imply that other drivers are unimportant. First we examined the evolving influence of service user knowledge and suggested that the social model was a significant outcome which has moved forward understandings within social work. We then suggested that the increasing trend towards personalisation was a derivative of the social model and speculated on how influential personalisation may become as a preferred method of service delivery. Second, we discussed interprofessional practice and looked at how knowledge has evolved as a result of the move towards greater collaboration. Finally, we briefly looked at some of the issues identified by inquiries into failings in social care.

We hope that you have enjoyed this chapter. We also hope that you have taken active steps to think about skill 8, reviewing, re-evaluating and reformulating your own views. It may be that your views have changed as a result of critically reviewing this chapter. For example, you may feel that there needs to be a much greater emphasis on service user feedback or that the gaps identified by successive inquiries into high-profile failings in the social care system only provide a partial account. Equally, you may feel that our concluding remarks about specialisation are inaccurate. Either way, you need to decide for yourself which of those critical building blocks of knowledge are integral to the development of the profession.

In our next chapter we turn our attention to the production of formal knowledge and ask, what are the benefits and limitations of involving service users, carers, practitioners and students in formal research?

Further reading

Horner, N. (2009) *What is Social Work? Context and Perspectives* (3rd edition). Exeter: Learning Matters.

As you will have seen, we have drawn on Horner's text in the early part of this chapter as he provides a helpful discussion about the historical context of social work. You will find his book very informative as it looks at how social work has evolved and become formalised and consolidated as a profession.

Social Care Institute for Excellence (SCIE) (2007) *Developing Social Care: Service Users Driving Culture Change*. Knowledge Review 17. London: SCIE (**www.scie.org.uk/publications/knowledgereviews/kr17.pdf**).

This guide, developed by three organisations, Shaping Our Lives, National Centre for Independent Living and University of Leeds Centre for Disability Studies, is freely downloadable from the internet. This is a report on primary research that explored the literature and practice around service user participation and the extent to which it has brought change and improvement to social work and social care.

Stanley, N. and Manthorpe, J. (2001) Reading Mental Health Inquiries – Messages for Social Work. *Journal of Social Work*, 1 (1): 77–99.

This journal article examines the findings of a number of mental health inquiry reports published during the 1990s. The authors draw out the implications of these inquiry findings for social work services and practice. While we would always recommend that you read fully any inquiry reports related to your area of practice interest, this meta-analysis, from the field of mental health, enables us to more fully understand emergent themes and their importance for the knowledge base for practice.

5 How is knowledge produced?

Ian Mathews

Achieving a Social Work Degree

Exercises and content in this chapter will focus on

- skill 1 demonstrating understanding and application of theoretical ideas
- skill 2 comparing and contrasting different viewpoints and experiences
- skill 3 relating different views to underlying philosophies or ideologies
- skill 4 evaluating different perspectives and ideas

In addition its content is particularly relevant to the following Social Work Subject Benchmarks.

5.1.5 the place of theoretical perspectives and evidence from international research in assessment and decision-making processes in social work practice
the integration of theoretical perspectives and evidence from international research into the design and implementation of effective social work intervention, with a wide range of service users, carers and others
the processes of reflection and evaluation, including familiarity with the range of approaches for evaluating service and welfare outcomes, and their significance for the development of practice and the practitioner

5.2 as an applied subject at honours degree level, social work necessarily involves the development of skills that may be of value in many situations (for example, analytical thinking, building relationships, working as a member of an organisation, intervention, evaluation and reflection). Some of these skills are specific to social work but many are also widely transferable. What helps to define the specific nature of these skills in a social work context are:

- the relative weighting given to such skills within social work practice (e.g. the central importance of problem-solving skills within complex human situations)
- the specific purpose of skill development (e.g. the acquisition of research skills in order to build a repertoire of research-based practice)
- a requirement to integrate a range of skills (i.e. not simply to demonstrate these in an isolated and incremental manner)

Introduction

Often when we think about how and where knowledge is produced we make the assumption that this is the domain of 'white middle-aged men in white coats', principally academic staff or researchers situated in universities. Throughout this book, however, we have encouraged you to think critically and to consider that other perhaps less traditionally defined forms of knowledge are equally as valid as knowledge produced by research. For example, in Chapter 2 we introduced the typology devised by Pawson et al. (2003) which enabled us to explore knowledge generated by practitioners, service users and carers, the policy community and organisational knowledge, none of which needs necessarily to be produced within the confines of academia. In that chapter our emphasis was on the more informal aspects of knowledge, where experience was the key feature in the production of knowledge. In this chapter we revisit some of those themes, but this time concentrate on how stakeholders are increasingly involved in the formal production of knowledge through research. In particular we want to consider three groups of potential researchers: service users and carers, practitioners, and students.

Service user and carer research

The first group we want to consider is that of service users and carers. We have already argued that it is unwise to consider this group as being homogeneous or as having the same needs, aspirations and perspectives. In reality, service users and carers are a diverse set of people who are often lumped together for administrative or organisational reasons. Nonetheless, for the purposes of this section we will use this phrase as shorthand for those people who either use or come into contact with social care services.

As an introduction to your thinking, McLaughlin (2009) provides a useful summary of the benefits that derive from the participation of service users and carers in formal research activity.

- Service users can provide a different perspective. This is perhaps a matter of common sense but it does no harm to remind ourselves that there are many competing interpretations and perspectives within social care and that the value of lived experience should not be overlooked within research.
- Service users and carers can provide a greater depth and quality to research data. Their understanding of issues and their ability to 'get alongside' other service users in a way that academics or practitioners cannot is invaluable to data gathering and interpretation.
- Coupled with this, service users and carers can ensure that the questions posed by research are appropriate and understandable. Academics and practitioners sometimes use terminology and language which is divorced from the rest of society and service users can be helpful in rewording and rephrasing incomprehensible language.

- Service users can assist with the dissemination of results. This is an important point. The value of research undertaken in health and social care depends on its usefulness. Service users are ideally placed to pass on new knowledge and fresh insights to other service users.

These are some of the advantages of drawing on service user expertise in research. As always we need to be balanced and recognise that there might also be disadvantages, or constraints, that need to be considered when involving users and carers in research.

Critical thinking exercise 5.1

What do you think are the potential disadvantages of involving users and carers in social care research?

To return to McLaughlin (2009), he suggests that there are a number of issues that need to be considered; for example, the amount of time required to train and prepare service users and carers to become competent researchers. This should not be underestimated as there is a considerable body of knowledge and skill that needs to be acquired before research can be undertaken. If this training and background work are not thoroughly undertaken there is a real danger that a service user is being set up to fail. A consistent complaint over the years is that organisations that need to involve service users have not adequately prepared them and consequently their involvement has been little more than tokenistic (Warren 2007).

There is also the issue of ethics. We will be looking at ethical considerations a little later in this chapter, but we need to note that service users may personally know the subjects of the research or may have particular connections with a service or service provider. In these circumstances, a decision would have to be taken as to whether it was ethical for that person to be involved in the research. As a minimal requirement the issue of establishing appropriate boundaries and respecting confidentiality would require careful thought.

Finally, there is the enduring problem of remuneration which needs to be considered. Sometimes service users are dependent on benefits which may be adversely affected by receiving payment for work undertaken. This has been a consistent issue for many years both in education and in practice and often has been poorly handled. However service users and carers are rewarded it should be meaningful and reflect the level of expertise and engagement that they bring to the task.

The changing nature of involvement

So far in this chapter we have perhaps implied that service users and carers are only used in research as helpers to academic staff or that they only have a peripheral role to play in the production of formal knowledge. Certainly until relatively recently this would have been an accurate portrayal of their involvement. We would, however, like to suggest that there has been, and continues to be, a welcome redistribution of power and that users are now often fully involved in producing their own streams of research.

You may recall that in Chapter 4 we referred to the work of Arnstein (1969) who devised a 'ladder of participation' which is often used to trace the involvement of users from non-engagement through to full participation. We would argue that in research a similar incremental process can be detected. Historically service users and carers were merely the objects of research by others (Horner 2009). In recent decades, however, there has been the development of what is referred to as 'participatory research'. This is where users were offered the opportunity to participate, but were typically given little in the way of control, influence or power over what was being researched or how the research would be conducted (Beresford and Croft 2001). Over time service users have increasingly rejected the limitations of participatory research and have become more and more involved in commissioning, undertaking and controlling research. This process has been referred to as 'emancipatory research'.

Key idea 5.1: **The aims, values and emancipatory nature of service user-controlled research**

As with many concepts in social work, 'participatory' and 'emancipatory' are contested and there is disagreement as to their definition and value. **Turner and Beresford** (2005: vi) acknowledge the contested nature of the terminology but suggest that service user-controlled research, however it is understood, should be characterised by a number of attributes.

First, the aims of user-controlled research are that it should:

- empower service users and improve their lives, both through the process and purpose of research;
- be part of a broader process of creating social and political change;
- change relations within research production where the people who carry out the research and those who are the subject of the research relate to each other on much more equal terms;
- be based on social models of understanding and interpretation.

The key values and principles associated with user-controlled research are:

- empowerment;
- emancipation;
- participation;
- equality;
- antidiscrimination.

A number of ways in which such research can emancipate service users have been identified. For example:

- the redefinition of the experience of disabled people/service users in the face of academic distortion;
- challenging traditional research methods and developing new, emancipatory methods;
- describing and valuing the collective experience of disabled people/service users and service user movements;
- the evaluation of services undertaken by service users.

There are a number of statements and aspirations highlighted here by Turner and Beresford (2005) which require further analysis. As can be seen, the nature of service user research is very different to the traditional definitions of research that we have previously discussed. It feels much more democratic in character, less 'scientific' and far more able to use subjective lived experience as a positive basis for enquiry. Understandably service users also often want to see different results from research: outcomes which make a clear difference to their lives and to the experiences of other social care users, such as social change, improved service delivery, the valuing of their lived experience, and social justice. This perspective should resonate with social work, which explicitly claims values such as empowerment, inclusion, and anti-oppressive practice. Due to these commonalities there is a real opportunity for collaboration between practitioners and users in the production of knowledge.

However we choose to define service user involvement in research it is clear that there has been a tangible change in the way that users are regarded within the research community. Warren (2007: 16) suggests that service users have become increasingly active in the following aspects of research:

- identifying and prioritising research topics;
- commissioning research;
- developing and designing research;
- managing research projects and programmes;
- undertaking research activity;
- interpreting research findings;
- disseminating the results of research;
- providing training and support to other researchers.

Examples of service user research

In order to exemplify the nature of research activity undertaken by service users we would like you to consider two contrasting research projects.

Example 1: Relationships and sexuality for young people with learning difficulty

The Centre for Disability Studies at the University of Leeds has an established reputation for involving service users in research. Their website (**www.leeds.ac.uk/disability-studies**) contains an interesting list of past and current projects.

Talking about sex and relationships: the views of young people was a three-year research project which sought the views and experiences of young people, teachers and parents regarding sex and relationships for young people with learning difficulty. The project was conducted in collaboration with CHANGE, a national organisation for people with learning difficulty, and adopted an emancipatory approach to the research.

Of particular interest are the following points.

- People with learning difficulty led the planning of the project.
- People with learning difficulty are on the board of trustees at CHANGE.
- People with learning difficulty were employed to assist in conducting the research.
- A drama group comprised of young people with learning difficulties assisted in the project. A significant and integral part of the project was that the drama group would assist research participants to devise and deliver a play based on their own knowledge and experience. This would form a key part of the dissemination process.
- The project had a volunteer with learning difficulty who assisted the drama group every week.
- Parents with learning difficulties were specifically included as part of the research sample.
- People with learning difficulties contributed to the writing up of the research to ensure that it was understandable and accessible.
- Dissemination was principally aimed at young people with learning difficulties as it was essentially about them and affected their lives.

As can be seen, the research and the dissemination process of this research project meets many of the characteristics suggested by Warren (2007) that we previously highlighted. In particular, service users were involved in:

- identifying and prioritising the research topics;
- developing and designing the research;
- managing the research projects;
- undertaking the research activity;
- disseminating the results of the research;
- providing training and support to other people involved in the project.

Optional further study

Gaine (2010) provides a useful summary of the issues involved in the search for equality and the recognition of diversity in social work practice. Chapter 6 by **Colin Goble** is particularly useful as it challenges the reader to celebrate and affirm disabled people – a perspective which is often missing from academic literature.

Example 2: The experience of compulsory admission to psychiatric care

In 1999 five mental health service users were invited by Birmingham University to co-research with academic staff the impact of compulsory admission into psychiatric care on the lives of service users. The study interviewed 11 people who between them had been admitted to hospital on 40 separate occasions. Researchers analysed the 'careers' of service users in mental health systems, the relationships between users and workers, and the well-being of users on discharge from hospital. The research identified a number of core themes including the difference in staff attitudes to those patients who were 'sectioned' and patients who were hospitalised on a voluntary basis (**Glynn** 2004).

What is especially interesting about this account is that Glynn was admitted to hospital twice himself during the course of the research. Understandably these highly personal experiences helped to inform and guide the research in a way that would not have been attainable by any other means. Glynn acknowledges that conducting the research was personally a transformative experience for him. This insight is interesting as it corresponds with the aspiration noted by Turner and Beresford (2005) that we quoted earlier where an advantage of service user-controlled research was that it had the potential to empower service users and improve their lives. Equally, this example provides a link between drawing on the expertise of service users in undertaking formal research and using experience as a key component of knowledge production. The very personal insights of the five service users must have been an advantage as only they, within the team, could begin to understand how admission and the journey through psychiatry affected the user/patient.

Critical thinking exercise 5.2

Having considered these differing examples, think about how your organisation does or could involve service users in research. Are there opportunities to encourage 'emancipatory research' which are not being taken? What do you think are the reasons for this?

Practitioner research

The second group of potential researchers we want you to consider is practitioners. We would encourage you to consider the term practitioner in its widest sense as we want to use the term inclusively to refer to anyone who practises in a social care setting.

Critical thinking exercise 5.3

Why should practitioners involve themselves in research activity? What are the advantages of involving practitioners in research?

Fuller and Petch (1995) suggest a number of reasons why practitioners should undertake research.

First, they suggest that practitioners undertake research to enhance their professional understanding. They argue that such is the pace and complexity of contemporary social care that undertaking research can give the practitioner a broader insight into the professional task. It can provide a more global contextual understanding of issues and help to develop a more professional persona.

Second, it can assist the practitioner to critically engage with research findings that underpin and move forward policy or practice. Often research is seen as being an activity which is beyond the reach of the practitioner and conducted by people who are out of touch with practice. Conducting research can help to bridge these gaps and give a practitioner an awareness of the advantages and limitations of research.

Third, research and the expertise it generates enhances the individual and collective knowledge base of social work leading to better, more informed decision-making. Such activity also increases the standing of the profession, particularly with other professions such as nursing or medicine who have a more sustained interest in research.

Finally, practitioner research can be a value-led process which reasserts the validity of professional social work over managerialism, bureaucracy and the political processes that on occasions seem to overwhelm it. It represents an opportunity to reclaim the values and principles of social work through the rediscovery and restatement of those elements of practice which are integral to the profession. To paraphrase **Giroux** (1988), it is the role of the enquiring social worker to *engage in uncovering, confronting and resisting power.* Research can be seen as one way of accomplishing this calling.

There are also a number of advantages to involving practitioners in research, not least the proximity they have to practice issues and the real concerns of social work. Equally, practitioners often already possess some of the essential skills required to be effective researchers: for example, the ability to conduct and accurately record interviews, problem-solving skills and the ability to critically reflect on information.

Post-registration training and learning

There is, however, another very clear reason why practitioners could consider involvement in research. That is the requirement from the professional body that oversees social care, The General Social Care Council (GSCC), that in order to remain professionally registered, a practitioner has to complete and record a significant amount of post-registration learning.

What the GSCC says about research

The GSCC provides clear guidance regarding the need for practitioners to update their knowledge, skills and understanding through post-registration training and learning if they wish to continue practising as a registered social worker.

The following extract is taken from the 'Post registration learning' section of the **GSCC** website (**www.gscc.org.uk**).

> *Our registration rules specify the post-registration training and learning requirements that all registered social workers must meet.*
> *The rules state that:*
>
> - *every social worker registered with the GSCC shall, within the period of registration, complete either 90 hours or 15 days of study, training, courses, seminars, reading, teaching or other activities which could reasonably be expected to advance the social worker's professional development, or contribute to the development of the profession as a whole;*
> - *every social worker registered with the GSCC shall keep a record of post-registration training and learning undertaken; and*
> - *failure to meet these conditions may be considered misconduct.*
>
> *What sort of post-registration training and learning activities should I undertake?*
>
> *We realise there are many ways to continue to learn and develop as a social worker so we have deliberately avoided being too speci×c about the type of activities which will meet our requirements.*
>
> *We expect you to choose training and learning activities that:*
>
> - *will benefit your current employment;*
> - *will benefit your career progression;*
> - *reflect your preferred learning style; and*
> - *make the most of the learning opportunities available to you to form part of your wider professional development.*

For example, you may wish to:

- *arrange to shadow the work of a colleague in a related team or profession*
- *negotiate protected time to research latest policy and good practice developments in your field of practice; or*
- *undertake a piece of research related to your practice.*

As you will see from this advice, there is a clear intention that practitioners could undertake research as a means of fulfilling the requirements of post-registration training and learning. There is also coherence with the stipulation that training activity should 'benefit your current employer' as research, if correctly configured, should have clear benefits to an organisation. Equally, it may be wise to keep in mind the other suggestion that research activity may 'benefit your career progression'. In a competitive age where promotion is difficult to achieve, or even where retaining your post may be challenging, it is always useful to have additional skills to add to your curriculum vitae.

The difficulties of practitioner research

Despite the advantages we have listed and explicit encouragement from the GSCC, there may be reasons why it is difficult or even inadvisable for practitioners to engage in research. As with service users or carers, the workers' familiarity with a subject or service area may be a potential hindrance or a source of bias which may prevent them from being critical or even objective. This lack of objectivity may even unconsciously lead an in-house researcher to 'find what they want to find'. There is the well-known, possibly anecdotal, example of a leading cigarette manufacturer who commissioned research into the effects of smoking in the 1970s. Unsurprisingly, the research found that smoking was not at all harmful and could even have therapeutic benefits. While the researchers were not necessarily 'insiders' there was a clear expectation from those who commissioned the research that a certain predetermined outcome would be found.

Fuller and Petch (1995) add that sometimes practitioner-led research can reveal unwelcome truths about services, teams or colleagues which can lead to difficulty. In such circumstances, researchers can find themselves uncomfortably accountable to a range of competing stakeholders including colleagues, managers, service users and politicians. Another limitation is that, pragmatically, many practitioners are far too pressurised and overcommitted in their day-to-day job to be able to undertake non-essential activities like research. Given the pressures on managers, such as chronic staff shortages and difficulties in recruitment, it is unlikely that practitioner research will become a significant feature of social care. We would argue that this is to the detriment of the profession which needs practitioners with diverse abilities and enquiring minds who can drive forward the knowledge base of social work.

Examples of practitioner research

Despite these pressures and restrictions there are some excellent examples of research which has been conducted by practitioners. We will highlight just two, both of which are drawn from *Practice: Social Work in Action,* a journal of the British Association of Social Workers.

Example 1: Practitioner research into the role of the wider family in child protection

Pitcher, D. and Arnill, M. (2010) Allowed to be There: The Wider Family and Child Protection. *Practice: Social Work in Action,* 22 (1): 17–31.

Pitcher and Arnill undertook research into the role of the extended family in protecting vulnerable children who are in the care of their parents. Their methodology was straightforward and involved convening a focus group of practitioners from a range of agencies concerned with child protection. Participants were invited to discuss two differing examples from their own caseload; one where extended family had assisted in the child protection plan, and one where the family had not been successfully engaged. In the second half of the day two people who ran a local support group for families with experience of the child protection system were invited to contribute to the discussion. Following an initial analysis of the day, one author then took provisional findings and ideas to a meeting of the support group for further consideration and refinement. This process enabled the authors to produce the following 'pointers for practice'.

Has all the information been shared with the family? This highlighted the need for channels of communication between professionals and families to be clear and open, the necessity of sharing professional insights and knowledge with family members and, in turn, recognising the value of reciprocal information from the family.

What is this family's communication pattern? This was a recognition of the importance of family dynamics and relationship patterns and the influence these have on communication.

Am I taking into account the effect I am having on the way the family responds, and how information is understood? This highlighted the importance of an ability to understand the impact that professional involvement can have on a family.

Can I identify, with the family, how the situation with the child has affected different family relationships? It is important to have an understanding that different members within the family will be affected in different ways and that professional involvement will be open to a number of interpretations.

Both authors of this article are practitioners within children's services. Pitcher is a Family Court Adviser for CAFCASS (the Children and Family Court Advisory and Support Service) while Arnill manages a local authority Family Group Conference service.

As you can see, their research was based on their own professional expertise and an identified need to analyse and possibly extend the involvement of extended families in supporting vulnerable children. We hope that you can see the positive impact of this piece of practitioner research. In many ways the process, that is the sharing of knowledge between practitioners and the active involvement of family members, is as important as the knowledge and conclusions produced.

Example 2: Practitioner research into service users' experiences of dual diagnosis

Lawrence-Jones, J. (2010) Dual Diagnosis (Drug/Alcohol and Mental Health): Service User Experiences. *Practice: Social Work in Action*, 22 (2): 115–31.

Lawrence-Jones's starting point was a realisation, based on practice, that service users who experienced substance misuse issues and mental health problems rarely have the opportunity to 'tell their story'. Professional and academic accounts rarely incorporate the views of service users regarding service provision, the experience of being assessed by professionals, and the stigma and exclusion faced on a daily basis. In order to rectify this omission, Lawrence-Jones undertook a number of semi-structured interviews with service users drawn from a statutory multidisciplinary substance use agency. He then analysed the interviews and produced a set of conclusions which highlighted the need to develop a more integrated approach to service provision which holistically addresses the complex health and social care needs of service users.

There are a number of commonalities between the two examples we have used. Lawrence-Jones is a practitioner with a local authority Children's Services department who used previous employment experience as a foundation for his research. Consequently, he draws on existing expertise in a similar way to Pitcher and Arnill (2010). His research also adopted a straightforward approach which entailed talking to service users in a structured, formalised way. This is not to detract from this piece of research as it is clearly important to empower the voice of disadvantaged and disregarded service users, particularly those who are often viewed as being responsible for their own difficulties. As we have consistently implied throughout this book, there is a hierarchy within knowledge which explicitly grades the importance of knowledge according to its source. As Foucault (1980) suggests, some knowledge is often casually disregarded as being naïve or insufficient and certain groups within society have what he terms a 'subjugated discourse'. This we would argue is the case for a range of service users, not least those who misuse substances.

Both examples also demonstrate some of the advantages that practitioners possess when conducting research; for example, the ability to use established connections and contacts as a basis for research and the use of pre-existing skills such as group work skills and interviewing techniques. We hope that you can see from these two brief examples that practitioner research is possible and need not be overly complicated. Both examples demonstrate the value of research to the individual, to their employing organisation, and to the wider community who can all use the knowledge produced.

Optional further study

Hardwick and Worsley (2011) have produced an accessible guide to practitioner research which covers important topics such as ethics, methods and involving service users and carers.

While it is not commonplace for practitioners to be involved in research activity, other groups within social care are even more underrepresented. In our next section we turn our attention to the largely untapped potential of engaging students in research.

Students as researchers

In order to stimulate your thinking around this subject we would like you to consider the following question.

Critical thinking exercise 5.4

Why should students involve themselves in research activity? What are the advantages of involving students in research?

You may well have a sense of déjà vu here as we posed the same question in relation to practitioners and research. This repetition is deliberate as social work students are practitioners-in-waiting and may already be practising in an unqualified position either as a part-time worker or as a student on placement. Consequently, there are good reasons why we should consider students and practitioners as being on a professional continuum.

We would argue that there are a number of reasons why students could and should be involved in research. The first reason is pragmatic and echoes the section on practitioner research. It is possible that finding employment on qualification may be challenging, especially in difficult economic conditions. Students often need to have additional 'strings to their bow' in order to enhance their job prospects. The research you undertake as a student may also be a gateway to an academic career, particularly if you are able to pursue your interests into practice.

Second, we would argue that involvement in research and knowledge production can assist you to become a critical thinker. Engaging in research activity requires the development of a range of skills which you will find invaluable to your studies and professional practice. Examples include the ability to undertake a detailed literature review, the skill of analysis and the need to be objective when considering competing claims and evidence. Often students are driven by the question, 'What do I need to do to pass this course?' While this is understandable it is essential that universities produce graduates and practitioners who are equipped with a portfolio of skills, especially the ability to think creatively and analytically (Healey and Jenkins 2009).

In recent years this argument has evolved and there has been an emphasis on students and practitioners developing what has been called 'research mindedness'. This has been defined as

- an ability to critically reflect informed by knowledge and research;
- an ability to use research to inform practice which counters unfair discrimination, racism, poverty, disadvantage and injustice consistent with core social work values;
- an understanding of research and how it relates to and influences practice.

adapted from **Keen et al.** (2009)

A student or newly qualified worker who already possesses these skills can be a real asset to a team, which again emphasises the continuum between work undertaken at university and practice. You will also note that the emphasis on using research as a means of promoting anti-oppressive practice has strong connections with the concept of 'emancipatory research' which we highlighted with reference to service users.

The third reason is more philosophical and again poses a question about the basis of contemporary education. It could be suggested that the traditional model of teaching in universities views students as passive recipients, little more than 'empty vessels waiting to be filled' by the expertise and wisdom of their lecturers. This model sees students as taking no active part in their own education and as using pre-existing knowledge and research purely as a means to an end (Healey 2005). It could be argued that this view has been strengthened by the introduction of student tuition fees in some parts of the United Kingdom which has led to a more consumerist approach being adopted by students and their families who understandably demand value for money.

There is, however, an alternative to this model where students are seen as co-participants and where their contribution to knowledge production is encouraged and valued. This is particularly relevant to the teaching of social work where many students already work within social care or have relevant life experience to share. As lecturers we have to be comfortable with the fact that on occasions students will have more direct experience and knowledge of a subject than we will! Consequently, it seems unwise not to acknowledge and use this depth of knowledge as a resource in teaching and research.

Examples of student research

Students are increasingly being invited to become co-researchers with academic staff and are also taking an active part in sharing their knowledge and expertise with other students on social work programmes.

Here are two examples to consider:

Example 1: A reflective account of being a student on placement

Buck, J. (2007) Social Work Placements: A Student Perspective. *Journal of Practice Teaching and Learning, 7* (1): 6–12.

In this article Buck reflects on her experience of being a social work student on placement. She discusses a range of issues which are of importance including the styles of the practice educators she worked with, the way that her emotional resilience increased as a result of her placement experiences and the importance of the support that she received from other students.

In terms of research this article is interesting as it records the critical reflections of just one person. While it might be unwise to overextrapolate from the subjective views of one student, it is important that a student perspective on placement provision is heard and valued. Often placement issues are researched and analysed by university-based academics or practice educators. It could be argued that those people who are most affected by the work undertaken on placement, students and service users, rarely have the opportunity to voice their opinion as to 'how it was for them'.

Example 2: Evaluating a social work degree programme

Simpson, D., Mathews, I., Croft, A., McKinna, G. and Lee, M. (2010) Student Views on Good Practice in Social Work Education. *Social Work Education,* 29 (7): 729–43.

In this piece of research two students were recruited to assist in the co-evaluation of the University of Lincoln undergraduate social work degree programme. The main focus of the research was to identify if and how the course equipped and prepared students for the pressures of professional practice.

The students undertook interviews with fellow students towards the end of the course and also sought to reinterview them after they had completed a year in practice. The research identified which parts of the course had been particularly valued by students and conversely which modules had been less well received. To generalise, those modules which had a clear practice focus, for example, child development or safeguarding modules, were popular with students while those which were devoted to underpinning issues were seen as less relevant. A key finding, however, was that sometimes students did not see the relevance of a module, or particular aspects of teaching, until they had been in practice for some time.

These two examples are both concerned with evaluation: one is a personal perspective, while the latter involved seeking the views of others. In a wider sense, however, moving away from 'pure' research, students are increasingly being asked to engage in the wider process of knowledge production. For example, on the University of Lincoln social work degree programme final year students are invited to share their knowledge with level two students regarding placement issues such as gathering service user feedback and how to successfully end contact with users. Sometimes on placement students are asked by their practice educator to compile resource files, or to present on a topic at a team meeting, or to undertake a small piece of research which will benefit the organisation. All of this activity is valuable both as a learning opportunity and also as a way of developing and honing skills important to practice.

Research ethics

Any form of formal research will require ethical approval. That is, those who undertake the research will have to gain permission to proceed from a body such as an ethics committee. In university settings it is likely that individual schools or faculties will have their own committees who will examine the ethical dimensions of the proposed research. In practice, both local authorities and the NHS are also developing rigorous ethical requirements. The situation in the private and voluntary sector is perhaps less rigorous, but as a rule no research should be undertaken without approval being received from an ethics body.

The reasons for seeking ethical approval are

. . . to ensure that researchers do not engage in practices that exploit or harm service users, or collect information that does not contribute to answering the research questions. [Ethics committees] ... also see that the appropriate safeguards are in place for consent, confidentiality, anonymity and so on.

Payne (2009: 267)

Ethical approval is a safeguard for the research team as well as proving that your research is bona fide, and acts as a checklist to follow while the research is ongoing.

Ethical issues

There are a number of ethical issues that need to be considered when undertaking research. These include:

- seeking 'informed consent' from a participant before they become involved in research. All participants should understand the purpose of the research, how the information they supply will be treated, and why they have been asked to take part. Researchers need to ensure that the participant has freely agreed to take part and has the necessary capacity to make that agreement. Seeking informed consent is especially important in social work research as often the people who are subject to research will have little power and may be used to agreeing with authority figures. Equally, there are always additional issues of consent to consider when undertaking research with people with learning difficulties, mental health difficulties or with children (**Adams et al.** 2009b). In England, social care research that involves people lacking capacity must be reviewed by a recognised appropriate body under the Mental Capacity Act 2005. The Social Care Research Ethics Committee run by the Social Care Institute for Excellent (SCIE) is recognised by the Secretary of State for this purpose. Similar arrangements are in place in other parts of the United Kingdom under the administration of devolved parliaments;
- adhering to the principle of non-maleficence. Deriving from medical ethics this means 'first, do no harm' and reminds the researcher that all intervention has consequences. While no researcher deliberately sets out to cause harm it is possible that some research approaches or interviews, particularly if connected to emotive topics such as abuse, may cause pain to participants or lead to unforeseen actions. Researchers need to carefully consider what issues may arise from their research and have plans in place to minimise these and to assist participants affected by memories or feelings evoked by the process;
- maintaining confidentiality. Ordinarily all information gathered in research is guaranteed to be confidential. This may mean that names of participants, locations and distinguishing characteristics have to be anonymised. On occasions – if, for example, abuse or poor practice is uncovered – it may not be possible to ensure confidentiality as these issues will have to be disclosed to the appropriate authorities (**Wilson et al.** 2008);
- ensuring independence. The independence of research must be clear and any conflicts of interest or partiality must be explicit. This is particularly an issue for 'in-house' researchers and echoes many of the comments we have already made regarding bias and the need for objectivity.

Research should always be a thoughtful, planned process which fully acknowledges issues of power and inequality. Seeking ethical approval ensures the integrity of research and is an important component of quality assurance and ensures that you have considered the impact of research on participants and communities.

Chapter Summary

In this chapter we have considered how knowledge is produced by exploring the contribution of three groups of potential researchers as separate entities. This was a conscious position as we wanted to contrast the potential for research by these groups with the traditional view of research as an activity solely undertaken by professional academics based in universities (skill 2). This dichotomy is perhaps a little stark as in reality research is often undertaken as a collaborative venture between researchers with different backgrounds, all bringing their own perspectives, skills and knowledge to the investigative venture. Throughout the chapter we have attempted to be balanced in our comments by recognising that there are both opportunities and challenges for all of these groups when they are involved in research. Another feature of the chapter was that we provided examples of research which we hope may inspire you to undertake research activity of your own.

First, we considered the evolving nature of service user and carer research and suggested that this group was becoming increasingly involved in the production of knowledge. Often this is through the use of knowledge based on experience but there are signs that users and carers are becoming more research active. We also acknowledged that there are some issues which need to be considered with service user research, not least the issue of subjectivity and bias and the support/training needs that users may have.

Second, we examined the role of practitioner research and argued that there are a number of reasons why practitioners should conduct research, not least to meet the requirement from the GSCC to undertake post-registration training and learning. We also acknowledged that often busy professionals find it difficult to engage with research activity and that being an in-house researcher can lead to the uncovering of uncomfortable truths resulting in mixed loyalties on the part of the researcher (Fuller and Petch 1995). Nonetheless, despite these difficulties, we argued that social workers need to consider research as part and parcel of their everyday role.

We then considered student research and suggested that, akin to service user research, this was becoming more common and increasingly valued. You may remember that we also suggested that there were many similarities between students and practitioners, as habits developed during university days can advantageously transfer to practice. We also sought to highlight connections between emancipatory service user research and the search for anti-oppressive practice in professional social work (skills 1 and 3). These relationships are of some significance as we would argue that there is a need for collaboration in research and that to see the production of knowledge as being the domain of one group is self-defeating (skill 4). It is our hope that, as service users, practitioners and students become increasingly familiar with and involved in research, alliances will be formed which drive forward the research agenda. This is not to suggest that university-based research should necessarily be diminished but that overall the value and credibility of social work research would be increased.

Further reading

Turner, M. and Beresford, P. (2005) *User-Controlled Research: Its Meanings and Potential.* Final Report. Brunel University: Shaping our Lives and the Centre for Citizen Participation. Available to download from **www.invo.org.uk/pdfs/UserCon_Rptfinal%20web081205.pdf**

This document reports on a project established to find out more about the definition, nature and operation of user-controlled research. It examines the benefits of and barriers to user-controlled research and makes recommendations for the future.

Mitchell, F., Lunt, N. and Shaw, I. (2008) *Practitioner Research in Social Services: a Literature Review.* IRISS. Downloadable from **www.iriss.org.uk/files/iriss-practitioner-research-literature-review-summary-2009-01.pdf**

This is a useful summary literature review that explores the issue of practitioner research in social services. The review was one part of an evaluation programme commissioned by the Institute for Research and Innovation in Social Services (IRISS) with funding from the Scottish Government's Changing Lives Fund. This short summary document provides a wealth of information on the topic of practitioner research and raises some questions relating to the furtherance of practitioner research.

Keen, S., Gray, I., Parker, J., Galpin, D. and Brown, K. (eds) (2009) *Newly Qualified Social Workers: A Handbook for Practice.* Exeter: Learning Matters.

This edited collection of chapters covers a wide range of topics that will support social workers new to practice following qualification, but also students in the later practice learning experiences. Of particular relevance to your learning in this chapter is its coverage of continuing professional development and research-mindedness in practice.

6 Contemporary professional practice and the changing use of knowledge

Ian Mathews

Achieving a Social Work Degree

Exercises in this chapter will focus on

- skill 1 demonstrating understanding and application of theoretical ideas
- skill 2 comparing and contrasting different viewpoints and experiences
- skill 5 evaluating evidence

In addition its content is particularly relevant to the following Social Work Subject Benchmarks.

4.7 learning to think critically about the complex social, legal, economic, political and cultural contexts in which social work practice is located

5.1.2 the service delivery context which includes the issues and trends in modern public and social policy and their relationship to contemporary practice and service delivery in social work

Introduction

As we have stated on a number of occasions in this book, social work is a dynamic, fast-moving profession whose knowledge base is open to challenge and change. In this chapter we want to start by returning to some of these arguments before progressing to an analysis of the impact that recent changes in the profession, and proposals for change, may have on the knowledge base of the profession.

The future of knowledge-informed practice

While some of these comments may be speculative it is interesting to see how current trends in the use of knowledge and changes within social work point towards the future. For example, Payne and Askeland (2008) in their discussion of the effects of globalisation argue that what may be regarded as sound social work knowledge in a UK context is irrelevant or even oppressive outside of the national context. They argue that the knowledge-producing educational and training systems of the UK are based on postcolonial assumptions which assume and propagate a certain world view; one which is culturally and geographically specific. Globalisation and the migration of skilled workers, particularly within the European Union and the West, mean that UK-trained social workers are now able to seek employment in many other countries. Conversely, many UK local authorities, especially those which have recruitment and retention difficulties, are often dependent on employing staff from overseas. This fluidity of employment means that social workers are taking 'their' knowledge with them to other parts of the world where very different cultures, expectations, assumptions and ways of working may mean that their knowledge is lacking in relevance or even redundant. Many UK social work courses now incorporate some teaching about international social work and the effects of globalisation, but it will be interesting to see how the employment patterns of social work impact on the content and structure of training programmes.

In terms of employment patterns, we could also argue that historically social work courses have made the assumption that graduates will work within the statutory sector and that the knowledge, skills and values taught on courses have reflected this assumption. With the economic uncertainty within the UK and the fiscal pressures on local authorities it may well be that increasing numbers of graduates seek employment within the private, voluntary and independent sectors. Again these changing patterns of employment call into question the appropriateness of the knowledge taught within universities. For example, it is rare that universities teach about the needs of voluntary organisations, such as writing bid proposals, managing budgets or training volunteers. While it is speculative, it may be that there needs to be a radical change in the knowledge basis of contemporary social work education in order to make it more fit for purpose in a rapidly changing work environment.

Throughout this book we have argued that we need to acknowledge that those elements of knowledge which are considered to be fundamental to social work practice are subject to change and evolution over time. This is hardly a radical thought as all academic subject areas and professional training courses need to ensure that they 'move with the times' and reflect changes within contemporary society and the evolution of our understanding as to how the world and society works. Parton (2008), however, in his review of the use of knowledge in practice, reminds us that social work was essentially a product of the nineteenth century. As such it did, and still does, have a variety of functions which straddle the hinterland between 'care' and 'control'. He argues that the traditional knowledge base derived from social sciences such as psychology and sociology has been progressively displaced by a *database form of knowledge* (2008: 264) reliant on computerised systems which increasingly seem to direct social work intervention.

There are other similar critiques of the use of knowledge within social work which we have previously analysed. For example, in Chapter 3 we précised the argument of Singh and Cowden (2009) who suggest that social work has undergone a process of 'de-intellectualisation' over recent decades. Successive governments have emphasised the more controlling aspects of the role where the professional is required to provide a service that 'works' but there is no attempt to explain (or address) the underlying issues that have brought service users to the attention of social workers in the first place. They argue in a similar way to Parton (2008) that social work has been reduced to a technical process devoid of any critical activity which would raise questions about the basis of practice. In their view social work has been successively reduced by government from being a progressive profession capable of challenging injustice and oppression to one that meets government performance targets, treats users as customers, and accepts restrictive financial budgets. Crucially, from this perspective, social workers are no longer encouraged to theorise, intellectually critique their role, or to use knowledge as a means of emancipation.

While these academic reviews and critiques are interesting and pose some profound questions about the nature of the profession, it could be argued that they are often written by people who are distant from practice and have limited power to move forward the debate. In our next section we begin an analysis of some of the policy drivers and agencies, often established by government, which do have the power to radically alter the profession and amend the knowledge base of social work.

Contemporary influences on the knowledge base of social work

Given the breadth, depth and increasing complexity of knowledge that social workers are expected to have, as well as the enormity of the professional task, it is not surprising that some newly qualified workers, especially those with limited life and work experience, sometimes find it difficult to make the adjustment from being a student to functioning as a fully fledged social work practitioner. Keen et al. (2009) refer pithily to this transition in their chapter title, 'Mind the gap'. How best to manage and support newly qualified staff has been a consistent problem within the profession for many years. In past times, it has been a perception among some social workers that some employers have been poor at offering supervision to newly appointed staff, have placed too many organisational and work pressures on them, and that managers have allocated cases to them which have far exceeded their ability to cope. Consequently, there has been a history of 'burnout' and 'dropout' among newly qualified social workers which has exacerbated many of the pressures that led to such poor managerial practice in the first place.

CASE STUDY

Mary is a recently appointed social worker in your organisation. She is in her early twenties, newly qualified, and seems to have only limited experience of working in social care. What formal sources of support are available to her in your agency during her first year of practice?

Clearly your responses will vary, as much will depend on context and whether you are working in the private, voluntary, independent or statutory sector. Managerial style and the service user group you work with will also exert an influence. Nonetheless, there are a range of formal supports that should be available to workers like Mary, not least supervision from her line manager (as discussed in Chapter 3). There are, however, other wider systems that have been introduced to guide and support workers like Mary. They are still evolving and taking shape; we discuss some examples here.

The Newly Qualified Social Worker framework

Partly in response to concerns about the difficulty of bridging the gap between qualification studies and professional practice, and the pressures generated by high-profile childcare cases such as the death of Peter Connelly in 2007 (Haringey Safeguarding Children Board 2009), the government introduced the Newly Qualified Social Worker (NQSW) framework in children's services in 2008, and into adult care a year later in 2009.

Optional further study

The NQSW framework and guidance on the outcome statements for both Children's Services and Adult Care is freely available on the internet. Childcare workers can download a copy of the *NQSW Outcome statements and guidance, Newly Qualified Social Worker Programme* at **www.cwdcouncil.org.uk**. Adult care workers can access a Newly Qualified Social Worker (NQSW) resource pack at **www.skillsforcare.org.uk**.

The purpose of the NQSW framework is to offer support, supervision and mentorship, as well as a protected caseload, to newly qualified workers during the first year or so of practice. The new practitioner is required to compile a portfolio of evidence in response to a range of key criteria which demonstrates their professional development and increasing competency. As such, the framework builds on the Personal Development Plan and progress file which social work students are required to complete during the last few months of their university training course. Arguably then for the first time there is a sense of cohesion between what has been studied at university and what needs to be learnt in practice.

The NQSW framework remains a pilot programme and is not currently available to all practitioners but has become an important means of supporting and equipping social workers. Methods and systems of supporting and assessing newly qualified workers will undoubtedly change and evolve in the next few years. For example, the Social Work Reform Board is currently exploring the possibility of introducing an 'assessed and supported year in employment' (ASYE) for all new practitioners. The purpose of the ASYE would be to offer the same level of support and supervision currently available within the NQSW framework, but would more formally assess the capability of the worker during their first year of employment before permitting them to continue with their career. The current intention is for AYSE to be introduced in pilot form as early as 2012 and for it to replace existing arrangements.

The NQSW outcomes

One of the purposes of the NQSW framework is to establish 'outcome statements' that 'set out national expectations for the professional skills, knowledge and abilities that NQSWs should attain by the end of their first year in employment' (**www.scie.org.uk**).

There are a range of outcomes which are common to workers in both children's services and adult care. These are:

- professional relationships;
- communication;
- referral;
- assessment;
- planning and intervention;
- review;
- recording and sharing information;
- multi-agency working;
- professional development and accountability.

Adult care workers also need to meet the following outcomes:

- safeguarding;
- service development;
- community capacity building.

www.scie.org.uk

Workers in children's services must also meet the following outcomes:

- formal meetings;
- disadvantaged groups.

Children's Workforce Development Council (CWDC 2010)

In order to see what these statements tell us about the use of knowledge in practice, we will now examine an outcome common to both adult care and children's services; that of 'planning' (which is entitled 'planning and intervention' in the adult care outcome statements).

Critical thinking exercise 6.1

Consider the scoping information outlined in the two outcome statements below. Make a list of the areas of knowledge which social workers are expected to demonstrate in order to meet the requirements of these outcomes.

Adult care 'Outcome statement 5, Planning and intervention'

Scope:

Plan, deliver, manage and commission person centred interventions at different levels of complexity (directly, as a team member, alongside others and through others), which focus on the individual's wishes and preferences, whilst taking into account the wishes and preferences of families and carers. Interventions must, within legal safeguards, impose control up to and including restrictions on liberty when behaviour presents a danger to the individual or other people, as well as ensuring equity in the rationing and allocation of scarce resources. They must balance the management of risk with individual dignity, choice and quality of life, encourage self directed care and maximise the control individuals have over their lives.

www.skillsforcare.org.uk

Children's services 'Outcome statement 3, Planning'

Scope:

The information you gather and analyse during an assessment provides you with the basis for planning the support and types of intervention required to improve outcomes for children and young people. It is important that these plans have clear objectives, based on planned outcomes for the child or young person, that they are agreed by the various parties involved, the process for their implementation is clear and that they have regular review points and are amended as necessary. As in all other aspects of your work, you will need to ascertain the wishes and feelings of individual children and young people. They should be consulted about actions and decisions because these will fundamentally affect their lives. The way you consult with them will be dependent on their age and understanding. Children and young people with disabilities may need additional support to ensure that their wishes and feelings are fully understood and taken into account.

You should work with parents in an open and collaborative way whenever possible. When parents have disabilities, appropriate communication methods should be used, ensuring personalised support that maximises their opportunity to parent their children. You will also need to recognise the different ways to work with parents and children and young people, taking account of diversity and cultural differences. However, no culture sanctions abusive parenting or care giving.

> *There may be circumstances where it is not possible to work collaboratively with parents or carers, in which case your decision to work in other ways should be justified and recorded. You will need to prepare plans in a range of circumstances and it is important that you are aware of the specific issues that these raise.*
>
> **CWDC** (2010: 11–12)

The outcome statements are, of course, much fuller than the brief information we have provided here and give far greater detail about the policy background and the breadth of knowledge, skills and values required to demonstrate capability in this area of practice. Nonetheless, the information provides at a least a snapshot of some of the key areas of knowledge required. It is difficult to second guess what your response was to this exercise, but here is our analysis of a number of broad themes common to both outcomes.

First, both outcome statements acknowledge that an explicit understanding of risk is required. Outcome 3 provides a description of some of the risk factors within families that workers in children's services may encounter; for example, children who experience 'domestic violence, substance misuse, mental ill health, living in workless families, in poverty or temporary accommodation', as well as issues around disability, asylum and teenage parenthood. Outcome 5 for adult care workers talks about the management of risk and the need to 'impose control . . . when behaviour presents a danger to the individual or other people'. As can be seen, there is an expectation that (even) newly qualified social workers will have gained knowledge about a significant range of social circumstances. The expectations incorporated within these outcome statements concisely demonstrate the complexity and breadth of knowledge that social workers are routinely expected to assimilate in contemporary practice. Additionally, NQSWs need to have gained an ability to make balanced and proportionate judgements about the level of risk that these behaviours and situations pose for vulnerable people. This is far from easy as 'risk' is a contested, fluid concept which cannot always be readily understood or assessed. To return to a familiar theme, this key task sometimes becomes easier with experience and the accumulation of 'practice wisdom'. Nonetheless, the level of nuances contained simply within this one area of current practice reinforces the need for the NQSW framework as a means of consolidating initial learning, developing the knowledge base and assisting newly qualified social workers to make sense of the complexity of the task they face.

The assessment of risk and other relevant factors, however, is only the beginning of the process and is purely a means of preparing the way for planned intervention. The notion of planning is explicit within both outcome statements and is the next commonality we need to discuss. There are many models of intervention which seek to guide social work practice and in order to assist our analysis we would like you to consider the following stage theory of intervention.

An example of a model of intervention

1. Immediate response and risk assessment;
2. Establishing rapport based on genuineness and respect;
3. Defining the major problems;
4. Encourage an exploration of feelings and provide support;
5. Consider alternative responses to the crisis;
6. Develop and implement an Action Plan;
7. Provide follow-up support plan and agreement.

adapted from **Roberts** (2000)

As can be seen from this model drawn from 'crisis intervention', intervention commences with assessment and then evolves through a number of stages leading to an end process characterised by forward planning.

It is interesting that the sequences alluded to in the outcome statements closely parallel the stages outlined by Roberts (2000). Outcome statement 3 advises that childcare workers need to 'gather' and 'analyse' information (stage 1) in ways that 'ascertain the wishes of children and young people' and their families (stage 2). Workers then need to formulate 'clear objectives' and 'planned outcomes' based on an identification of the major issues (stage 3). 'Wishes and feelings are fully understood and taken into account' (stage 4) while preparing plans to address a range of circumstances (stage 5). Finally, the guidance advises that the process for the implementation of plans is clear; they are regularly reviewed and are open to change (stages 6 and 7) (CWDC 2010). A similar exercise could be readily undertaken with outcome statement 5 as this statement has an even greater emphasis on moving forward to intervention. Without wishing to labour the point, these processes demonstrate the breadth of knowledge required by workers and show the interface that exists between skills, knowledge and values.

Another commonality we noticed between these outcome statements is the emphasis that is placed on the more controlling aspects of social work. Outcome 3 talks about working in partnership and reaching agreement with the various stakeholders involved in the welfare of the child but concludes, 'there may be circumstances where it is not possible to work collaboratively with parents or carers' (CWDC 2010). It is at this point that the social worker needs to justify their intervention but also act in a decisive manner that puts the interest of the child first. Outcome statement 5 for adult care workers is even more explicit, talking about the need for intervention to 'impose control' and if required to 'restrict liberty'. We have spoken of the dichotomy that exists between 'care' and 'control' within social work on a number of occasions in this book and do not intend to restate the issues again. Suffice to say, it is interesting to see the need for control explicitly stated and to again consider the breadth and depth of knowledge required to make legal and proportionate decisions that impose control on people and situations.

A final commonality is the encouragement to work in a collaborative way with other professionals in other agencies. While this is implicit in the scoping statements we have quoted – for example, the directive that adult care workers operate 'alongside others and through others' – it is more explicitly stated in the rest of the wider statement. Again this is not a surprise as social work operates in a multi-agency, interprofessional arena where few major decisions are taken without comprehensive reference to others. Social workers in contemporary practice then need to have knowledge of the culture, values, roles and training of other professionals as well as knowledge of how to access support and information. The worker then needs to know how to process the information and how to interpret the often differing messages that it contains.

To summarise, we have used one common element from the NQSW outcome statements to make a range of points regarding the role of knowledge, and what practitioners are expected to know, in contemporary practice. Unsurprisingly, there are considerable commonalities between the knowledge required in different areas of work and it is salutary to consider that this breadth and depth of knowledge is expected to have been acquired by social workers by the end of their first year in practice.

The NQSW pilot programmes are designed to provide structure and support at a crucial time in professional development but are purely one component part in the government's plan to modernise social work training and education. We now move forward to consider another powerful driver that will potentially introduce wide-ranging change to the profession.

The Social Work Reform Board

In 2008 the Government established the *Social Work Task Force*, chaired by Moira Gibb, to conduct a review of the profession and to advise on a comprehensive reform programme for social work. The task force produced its final report (HM Government 2009) in December 2009. This provided a set of 15 far-reaching recommendations; these are being taken forward by the *Social Work Reform Board*. A key recommendation in a follow-up report one year on was 'the creation of a single, nationally recognised career structure for social workers' (HM Government 2010: 6), which established clear expectations of what social workers should know and be able to do at each stage of their career. In order to facilitate this development, the Social Work Reform Board has proposed the creation of a 'Professional Capabilities Framework for Social Workers in England' which will influence key aspects of development such as education and training, continuing professional development and performance management (HM Government 2010: 7).

We have chosen to include the full list of proposed professional capabilities as they again show the breadth of knowledge that contemporary workers will be expected to demonstrate. In a similar way to the NQSW framework, they also exemplify the connection between knowledge, skills and values which underpins professional practice.

Proposed Professional Capabilities Framework for Social Workers in England

The proposed capabilities are:

Professionalism – Identify and behave as a professional social worker, committed to professional development

Social workers are members of an internationally recognised profession, a title protected in UK law. Social workers demonstrate professional commitment by taking responsibility for their conduct, practice and learning, with support through supervision. As representatives of the social work profession they safeguard its reputation and are accountable to the professional regulator.

Values and Ethics – Apply social work ethical principles and values to guide professional practice

Social workers have an obligation to conduct themselves ethically and to engage in ethical decision-making, including through partnership with people who use their services. Social workers are knowledgeable about the value base of their profession, its ethical standards and relevant law.

Diversity – Recognise diversity and apply anti-discriminatory and anti-oppressive principles in practice

Social workers understand that diversity characterises and shapes human experience and is critical to the formation of identity. Diversity is multi-dimensional and includes race, disability, class, economic status, age, sexuality, gender and transgender, faith and belief. Social workers appreciate that, as a consequence of difference, a person's life experience may include oppression, marginalisation and alienation as well as privilege, power and acclaim, and are able to challenge appropriately.

Rights, Justice and Economic Wellbeing – Advance human rights and promote social justice and economic wellbeing

Social workers recognise the fundamental principles of human rights and equality, and that these are protected in national and international law, conventions and policies. They ensure these principles underpin their practice. Social workers understand the importance of using and contributing to case law and applying these rights in their own practice. They understand the effects of oppression, discrimination and poverty.

Knowledge – Apply knowledge of social sciences, law and social work practice theory

Social workers understand psychological, social, cultural, spiritual and physical influences on people; human development throughout the life span and the legal framework for practice. They apply this knowledge in their work with individuals, families and communities. They know and use theories and methods of social work practice.

Critical Reflection and Analysis – Apply critical reflection and analysis to inform and provide a rationale for professional decision-making

Social workers are knowledgeable about and apply the principles of critical thinking and reasoned discernment. They identify, distinguish, evaluate and integrate multiple sources of knowledge and evidence. These include practice evidence, their own practice experience, service user and carer experience together with research-based, organisational, policy and legal knowledge. They use critical thinking augmented by creativity and curiosity.

Intervention and Skills – Use judgement and authority to intervene with individuals, families and communities to promote independence, provide support and prevent harm, neglect and abuse

Social workers engage with individuals, families, groups and communities, working alongside people to assess and intervene. They enable effective relationships and are effective communicators, using appropriate skills. Using their professional judgement, they employ a range of interventions: promoting independence, providing support and protection, taking preventative action and ensuring safety whilst balancing rights and risks. They understand and take account of differentials in power, and are able to use authority appropriately. They evaluate their own practice and the outcomes for those they work with.

Contexts and Organisations – Engage with, inform, and adapt to changing contexts that shape practice Operate effectively within own organisational frameworks and contribute to the development of services and organisations. Operate effectively within multi-agency and inter-professional settings

Social workers are informed about and pro-actively responsive to the challenges and opportunities that come with changing social contexts and constructs. They fulfil this responsibility in accordance with their professional values and ethics, both as individual professionals and as members of the organisation in which they work. They collaborate, inform and are informed by their work with others, inter-professionally and with communities.

Professional Leadership – Take responsibility for the professional learning and development of others through supervision, mentoring, assessing, research, teaching, leadership and management

The social work profession evolves through the contribution of its members in activities such as practice research, supervision, assessment of practice, teaching and management. An individual's contribution will gain influence when undertaken as part of a learning, practice-focused organisation. Learning may be facilitated with a wide range of people including social work colleagues, service users and carers, volunteers, foster carers and other professionals.

HM Government (2010: 10–11)

Critical thinking exercise 6.2

Consider the professional capability entitled 'Critical reflection and analysis'. What does it tell us about the analytical skills that social workers are required to demonstrate in practice?

It is interesting to see the language that is used in this professional capability. First, social workers are expected to know about and apply higher-level critical analysis and something called 'reasoned discernment'. This latter term is not (as yet) defined but seems to have at least a link to some of the arguments we have précised regarding 'practice wisdom'.

There is then an explicit acknowledgement that social workers rely on and use knowledge from a range of sources, including 'their own practice experience'. You may have noted that the other sources identified – 'service user and carer experience together with research-based, organisational, policy and legal knowledge' – bear a clear resemblance to the SCIE classification we have consistently used in this book developed by Pawson et al. (2003).

Second, this capability places an onus on the need to 'identify, distinguish, evaluate and integrate' sources of knowledge. These analytical skills are clearly of importance to effective practice and connect to a number of themes within this book. For example, in Chapter 3 we traced the evolution of reflective practice and explored ways to interrogate knowledge within professional supervision. In many ways the words used here are simply encouraging social workers to analyse possible sources of knowledge and to adopt a critical stance to evidence. This further corresponds to another section in Chapter 3 where we highlighted the work of Pawson et al. (2003) and the use of the acronym TAPUPA as a means of assessing the validity of knowledge. You may recall that TAPUPA stands for transparency, accuracy, purposivity, utility, propriety and accessibility. Again there is a clear comparison to be made as this is another method of 'identifying, distinguishing, evaluating and integrating' sources of knowledge.

A number of the other proposed capabilities make reference to aspects of knowledge or evidence. We have summarised these in Table 6.1.

Table 6.1: The professional capabilities framework and knowledge

Professionalism – Identify and behave as a professional social worker, committed to professional development	Social workers 'demonstrate professional commitment by taking responsibility for their . . . learning'. They also need to know about accountability and how this impacts on practice and conduct
Values and Ethics – Apply social work ethical principles and values to guide professional practice	Social workers are required to make 'ethical decisions' in 'partnership' with service users. They are required to demonstrate knowledge about the value base of the profession, its ethical standards and legal basis
Diversity – Recognise diversity and apply anti-discriminatory and anti-oppressive principles in practice	Social workers need to know about a range of human factors including race, disability, class, economic status, age, sexuality, gender and transgender, faith and belief. Additionally, they need to know how to work with difference and diversity and how to fight against oppression and discrimination
Rights, Justice and Economic Wellbeing – Advance human rights and promote social justice and economic wellbeing	Social workers need to know about, and have the ability to put into practice, the principles of human rights and equality as established by a range of law- and policy-making bodies
Intervention and Skills – Use judgement and authority to intervene with individuals, families and communities to promote independence, provide support and prevent harm, neglect and abuse	Social workers need to know how to work with people and how to effectively assess their needs and plan interventions
Contexts and Organisations – Engage with, inform, and adapt to changing contexts that shape practice. Operate effectively within own organisational frameworks and contribute to the development of services and organisations. Operate effectively within multi-agency and inter-professional settings	Social workers need to know about the organisational context within which they work and have the ability to respond flexibly to change. They require knowledge about other organisations and professional contexts and need to work effectively across boundaries – and settings
Professional Leadership – Take responsibility for the professional learning and development of others through supervision, mentoring, assessing, research, teaching, leadership and management	Social workers have a responsibility to pass on their knowledge to others and to share their expertise using a variety of methods such as supervision, mentoring and management

Critical thinking exercise 6.3

You may have noted that we have deliberately omitted reference to the proposed capability regarding 'knowledge'. We would like you to consider this capability now and compare it with your own knowledge. Is it true, for example, 'that social workers understand psychological, social, cultural, spiritual and physical influences on people'?

As a reminder, here is the proposed capability on knowledge:

Knowledge — Apply knowledge of social sciences, law and social work practice theory

Social workers understand psychological, social, cultural, spiritual and physical influences on people; human development throughout the life span and the legal framework for practice. They apply this knowledge in their work with individuals, families and communities. They know and use theories and methods of social work practice.

(**HM Government** 2010: 11)

This exercise is essentially a personal audit of your own knowledge base which will reflect your training, your post-qualification experience and practice setting. Consequently it is difficult to make general comments as responses will be very different. Nonetheless, there are a number of statements within the capability which are of interest: for example, the assumption that social workers know about the social sciences. You may remember that at the commencement of this chapter we referred to the work of Parton (2008) who argues that the traditional social sciences knowledge base of social work has been eroded and replaced by IT systems which now drive decision-making. In his argument there is little room for the type of analysis that derives from knowledge of psychology, sociology and social policy. It would be interesting to see your response to this argument. As a personal observation, while the theory and ways of thinking that characterise the social sciences may implicitly guide social work training there are few qualifying courses that explicitly offer modules on sociology, psychology, etc.

Equally, it is possible to critique the statement that social workers understand spiritual influences on people. While interest in spirituality continues to grow, especially in mental health, there is an argument that social workers do not recognise the spiritual needs of service users and are uncomfortable working with this aspect of life (Moss 2005). The following extract from *Social Work and Spirituality* (Mathews 2009) further explores this thought.

Many of you reading this book will be undertaking a social work qualification course, or will be newly qualified. I imagine that what you were taught at university remains fresh in your mind. Significant elements of it would be based on traditional disciplines within the social sciences – sociology, social policy and psychology. All of those disciplines are secular and often have little sensitivity towards faith or religion. For example, the German sociologist Karl Marx, whose work has inspired and informed radical social work for many generations, describes religion as being the *opiate of the masses*, and *pie in the sky when you die*. Other influential sociologists, such as Max Weber and Emile Durkheim,

> recognised the importance of religion but predicted in a modern world with enlightened views that it would become extinct. In psychology, Sigmund Freud, the father of the psychoanalytical approach, viewed religion in a number of ways – none of them complimentary. For example, religion was a mass delusion, a reaction to infantile helplessness, or a form of paranoia.
>
> In other subject areas, such as mental health, it is common to hear how mentally distressed people in former years were deemed to be possessed by the devil, or were being punished by God for their wrongdoings.
>
> In social policy, the role of the church in encouraging punitive legislation, designed to manage the poor and the rebellious from the Poor Law onwards, is often cited. The way the Anglican Church and the state were intertwined in past centuries leading to a domination of the educational system and an active shaping of the school curriculum is often portrayed as historically oppressive.
>
> It is not a surprise that social workers pick up on this hostility and tend to echo what they have been taught in practice. Often on social work courses there is no teaching on spirituality and no recognition of the role of faith to provide a more balanced perspective.
>
> Living as we do in a secular society where decreasing numbers of people attend a place of worship or profess any religious affiliation, it is uncommon to come across a health or social care worker who is entirely comfortable with religion — for the simple reason that few have an in-depth knowledge of religion, few attend a place of worship, and many express a disinterest, even antipathy, towards religion. As you read earlier in this chapter, sometimes service users feel unable to raise their spiritual needs due to the embarrassed response they may receive from workers. As Baskin (2002) states in relation to social work training the topic of spirituality is usually met with silence and the lowering of the eyes.
>
> This diffidence, I would argue, detracts from the vibrancy and validity of social work. Our lack of spiritual understanding and our inability to harness the tools that this would bring to our practice has led to nothing less than an impoverishment of social work.
>
> **Mathews** (2009: 16–17)

We do not assume that you accept this argument but it does touch on some interesting debates concerning the awareness of social workers and the difficulties some may have relating to the spiritual needs of service users or even entire faith communities. In a similar way we could also question the statement within this capability that 'social workers understand . . . cultural influences on people'. In the same way that many social workers would struggle to relate to all expressions of spirituality that exist in such a diverse society as the UK, it is also likely that few could claim to understand *all* the influences exerted by culture.

It is also significant that the capability framework emphasises that workers 'apply this knowledge in their work with individuals, families and *communities*'. This all-embracing phrase is frequently repeated throughout the standards that guide social work training and practice; for example, the National Occupational Standards, the GSCC Codes of Practice and the NQSW framework. While work with families and individuals is clear to see in contemporary social work practice, explicit work with communities is harder to discern. Many practitioners would claim that their work implicitly sustains and benefits community cohesion, but there is an argument that in recent decades social work has forsaken its roots in community action and has systematically distanced itself from community work Horner (2009).

Critical thinking exercise 6.4

If you have experience of working in a social care setting, either through employment or being on placement, think about your role and the work undertaken by your organisation. Make a list of concrete examples of ways in which you have directly worked with your local community.

If we had asked you to make a list of ways in which you had worked with individuals and families in recent weeks we suspect that your list could be extensive. Obviously, this will depend on your practice setting as there may well be local authority-employed community workers, or practitioners in the voluntary sector, reading this book who work all the time with communities. Nonetheless, the bulk of social work practice is with individuals and families and we would argue that direct social work with communities is relatively rare.

Finally, the notion that practitioners use theories and methods can be questioned. As we have already discussed in our analysis of 'practice wisdom' (in Chapter 2), often the explicit use of theory is difficult to see, especially in the work of busy practitioners who have process-driven deadlines to meet. Nonetheless, we would want to affirm the thoughtful and well-informed work that practitioners do and suggest that this professional capability could be used in supervision as a way of encouraging professional and critical reflection.

Chapter Summary

In this chapter we commenced by offering some speculative thoughts on the future of knowledge-informed practice in social work. We reminded ourselves that all professions and the knowledge that informs their work constantly evolve and move forward.

Sometimes this evolution occurs in ways that can be predicted and welcomed and on other occasions change is unexpected and piecemeal. In particular, we noted the influence of globalisation and how social workers are now in a position to export what they consider to be knowledge to different parts of the world or into different sectors of the economy within the UK. This discussion enabled us to raise some concerns about the validity of social work training and how 'fit for purpose' it is in a highly mobile world.

We then analysed the influence of new and pending frameworks which have been introduced to support newly qualified workers, in particular, the NQSW framework and the proposals to introduce a 'Professional Capabilities framework'. The latter will have a wider remit than the NQSW framework as over time the intention is to use the capabilities to make judgements about the capability of all social work practitioners regardless of where they are in their career.

Our analysis of these frameworks enabled us to make a number of key points.

- The breadth and depth of knowledge that social workers are required to know is considerable.
- Despite evident differences, there are also many commonalities between the knowledge required by adult care workers and workers in children's services. We highlighted three specific examples from the NQSW framework: the need to have an explicit understanding of risk; the ability to plan interventions; and the need to work in a collaborative way with others.
- As elsewhere in this book, we have concentrated on the knowledge that underpins practice, but would also want you to explicitly recognise the interconnection between knowledge, skills and values that exists in the examples we have used.
- There is a debate in contemporary practice and training as to the fundamental basis of professional education. We raised the issue of the role of the social sciences and noted that they were explicitly mentioned in the 'Proposed Capabilities Framework'.
- Finally, we raised questions about some of the assumptions that underpin both of the frameworks we discussed; for example, the suggestion that social workers know about the culture and spiritual needs of their service users and that they engage in community work.

The skills development elements of this chapter have centred on developing your ability to evaluate evidence. As we hope you will have understood as you have worked through this book, what we consider to be knowledge and how that knowledge is used is highly contested. Consequently, there are often few right answers and much is open to debate. The arguments we have presented in this chapter are all open to challenge and we hope that you have enjoyed the engagement.

In our final chapter we review the major themes of this book and encourage you to consolidate your learning by re-examining the fundamental principles that underpin evidence-based practice in social work.

Further reading

Parton, N. (2008) Changes in the Form of Knowledge in Social Work: From the 'Social' to the 'Informational'? *British Journal of Social Work*, 38 (2): 253–69.

This article explores the changing form of knowledge in social work over the past 30 years and its implications for theory and practice. As you have read in this chapter, Parton examines the impact of new information and communication technologies and the shift from a narrative to a database way of thinking and operating. Parton argues that such changes have implications for the relationship between theory and practice in social work and the nature of 'social' work itself.

Payne, M. and Askeland, G. A. (2008) *Globalization and International Social Work: Postmodern Change and Challenge*. London: Ashgate.

This book examines developments in international social work through the lens of postmodernism and globalisation. You will find Chapter 1 particularly relevant to your studies as the authors explore the development of a social work knowledge base.

Skills for Care www.skillsforcare.org.uk

Skills for Care is an employer-led authority on the training standards and development needs of people working in adult social care in England. Within the pages of their website, you will find the 'NQSW Resource Pack' with a range of freely downloadable documents, 'frequently asked questions', details about each of the outcome statements, supervision and continuing professional development.

Conclusion: Why is it necessary to consider the evidence and knowledge that underpins practice?

Karin Crawford

Achieving a Social Work Degree

Exercises and content in this chapter focus will on

- skill 2 comparing and contrasting different viewpoints and experiences
- skill 3 relating different views to underlying philosophies or ideologies
- skill 4 evaluating different perspectives and ideas
- skill 7 reflection
- skill 8 reviewing, re-evaluating and reformulating your own ideas

In addition its content is particularly relevant to the following Social Work Subject Benchmarks.

4.7 the ability to acquire and apply the habits of critical reflection, self-evaluation and consultation, and make appropriate use of research in decision-making about practice and in the evaluation of outcomes

5.1.5 the ability to acquire and apply processes of reflection and evaluation, including familiarity with the range of approaches for evaluating service and welfare outcomes, and their significance to the development of practice and the practitioner

5.2 as an applied subject at honours degree level, social work necessarily involves the development of skills that may be of value in many situations (for example, analytical thinking, building relationships, working as a member of an organisation, intervention, evaluation and reflection). Some of these skills are specific to social work but many are also widely transferable. The factors that help to define the specific nature of these skills in a social work context are:

- the relative weighting given to such skills within social work practice (e.g. the central importance of problem-solving skills within complex human situations)
- the specific purpose of skill development (e.g. the acquisition of research skills in order to build a repertoire of research-based practice)
- a requirement to integrate a range of skills (i.e. not simply to demonstrate these in an isolated and incremental manner)

Introduction

This chapter marks the end of our journey, which we hope you have found both enjoyable and stimulating. In this concluding chapter we have incorporated explicitly in the text reference to the skills we hope that you have been developing throughout your studies. In this way we aim to demonstrate that perhaps implicitly your ability to evaluate, analyse and critique has been incrementally improving during your studies. Additionally, in this final chapter of the book, you will also have the opportunity to consolidate your learning by reviewing the key themes that are threaded throughout each preceding chapter. The themes are listed below.

1) The use and development of evidence and knowledge, alongside values, ethics and skills, form the basis of effective social work professional practice.
2) Evidence and knowledge for social work practice needs to be subjected to critical reflection, scrutiny and interrogation to ensure it is relevant, reliable, trustworthy and contextually appropriate.
3) It is important to understand how knowledge that emanates from the views and perspectives of service users and carers provides an essential contribution to the research and knowledge that underpins and shapes ethical professional practice.

Therefore, this chapter, being structured around a discussion of each theme, summarises and reinforces the main issues that emerge across the chapters of this book, highlighting the connections between them. Additionally, the chapter offers a number of critical thinking review exercises for you to work through to further strengthen your learning and confirm your understanding. The chapter closes by re-examining the fundamental principles that underpin evidence-based practice in social work.

The use and development of evidence and knowledge, alongside values, ethics and skills, form the basis of effective social work professional practice

This is an overarching theme that underpins the whole ethos of this book and our motives for writing it. Within this theme we reinforce not only the importance of evidence and knowledge for social work practice, but also the responsibility that social workers have for generating and contributing to the professional knowledge base. Furthermore, we argue that there is a dynamic relationship between knowledge and our professional values and ethics, both being fundamental factors in the development of effective professional practice and anti-oppressive practice. Thus, as explored in Chapter 3, values are informed and influenced by knowledge while, in turn, values inform and influence the selection, critique and development of knowledge for practice. In reality social work practice is even more complex than this, being potentially a three-way interaction between knowledge and evidence, values and ethics, and skills; as illustrated in Figure 7.1.

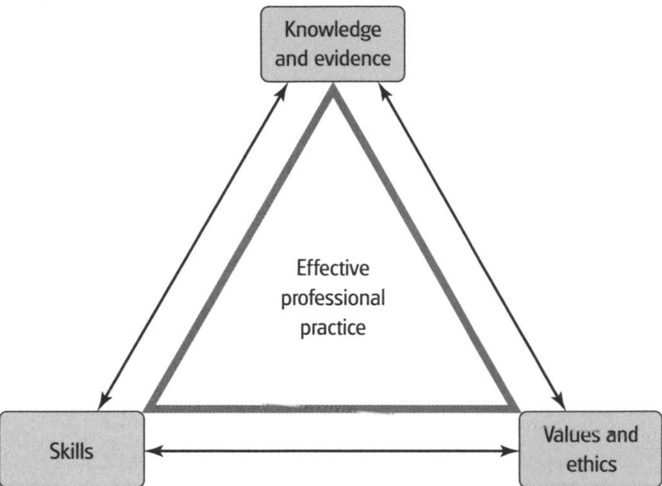

Figure 7.1: A model of three-way interaction of knowledge and evidence, values and ethics, and skills

The focus of this book then has been the contribution of knowledge and evidence to effective professional practice. In the early part of this book, particularly Chapter 1, we invited you to consider some of the distinctions between the key terms 'evidence' and 'knowledge'. We suggested that evidence results from a process of planned systematic enquiry (research), which is capable of producing empirical findings, and that those findings, or results, are applicable to a range of situations and people. In this paradigm, evidence is commonly viewed as being objective in nature and inherently reliable. Knowledge, however, is a much broader, complex construct with elements of ambiguity and uncertainty. It is less scientific in nature and is able to contain elements of subjectivity (Blom 2009). That is, the processes of 'doing', 'experiencing' and 'understanding' create and add to our knowledge. In other words, knowledge is 'made rather than revealed' (Taylor and White 2000: 199). This is a crucial distinction as it gives credibility to less formal knowledge constructions and enables us to recognise the inherent value of experience.

This 'fault line' between evidence and knowledge appears on a number of occasions in this book; for example, in our thinking regarding the different sources of knowledge that potentially underpin practice. In Chapters 2 and 3 we noted that there are a number of ways in which knowledge can be classified or categorised. Using the typology developed by Pawson et al. (2003) we introduced five possible sources:

- organisational knowledge, which is generated by managers and bureaucrats within organisations, typically through the management, oversight and governance of social care;
- practitioner knowledge, which arises from the experience, practice wisdom, tacit knowledge and reflective practice of those engaged in social care practice;

- policy community knowledge, which arises from the wider strategic and policy environment. This would include institutional reviews, audits, commissions and 'think tank' outputs;
- research knowledge 'gathered systematically with predetermined design', often by academic staff within universities, including empirical inquiries, evaluations and evaluative reports;
- user and carer knowledge, which arises directly from the lived experience and reflections of being a service user or carer.

Within this typology it is possible to see that some sources of knowledge (arguably service user, carer and practitioner knowledge) are more subjective and less scientific than others. Without wishing to overstate the argument, these sources may be less evidential in nature than categories such as research or policy community knowledge.

Trevithick (2007) also validated this division in her work on categorising knowledge as she offered an analysis of the different ideologies that underpin knowledge production. Implicit within these distinctions is the question: 'are some sources, or ways of producing evidence or knowledge, more important or more valuable to practice than others?' As Trevithick (2007) implies in her argument, scientific methods of producing and analysing evidence are often seen as being the 'gold standard', with other methods of producing knowledge being viewed, therefore, as less rigorous, more subjective and consequently second rate. Throughout this book, we have encouraged you to question the validity of that proposition using skills such as evaluation and the critical review of a range of competing perspectives (skill 4 and skill 8). Additionally in our society, scientific research is a multi-million-pound business that often receives government funding, favourable coverage in the media, and is emphasised as being something to aspire to in schools and universities; consequently the science community wields considerable power and influence. In contrast, other forms of research or enquiry often receive scant attention and considerably less funding. This division was also clearly apparent in the work of McLaughlin (2007) who categorises knowledge according to the way it is produced; the 'mode of production'. To generalise, he distinguishes between academic knowledge produced, constructed and owned by the academic community, and knowledge produced by experience and application. This second mode of production can be seen to equate to practice wisdom as it is produced by practitioners through application and experience 'in the field'.

The concepts of practice wisdom and practitioner knowledge and their potentially subjective natures form a key part of the discussion in Chapter 2. On the one hand these concepts, particularly 'practice wisdom', relate to the use of experiential learning, tacit knowledge and developed skills. On the other hand, however, as discussed in Chapter 5, practitioner knowledge is developed and enhanced through practitioner research, or formal explicit enquiry into practice and service effectiveness. Formalised practitioner research is being increasingly encouraged within postgraduate and post-qualifying education and more widely through social care organisations who are not only motivated to support individuals' professional development, but also keen to enhance services through critical engagement with practice-led research. Later in this chapter, following discussion about the place of service user research, you will have the opportunity through a critical thinking exercise to reflect on the similarities and differences between knowledge that emerges from the work of practitioners and knowledge that emerges from the experiences and perspectives of service users. This will enable you to develop further your ability to compare and contrast different viewpoints and experiences (skill 2). The following exercise, however, has been constructed to support you in consolidating your learning about the significance of evidence and knowledge for professional social work practice.

Critical thinking exercise 7.1: Evidence and knowledge for social work practice

Reflect on your experience of social care or social work practice, perhaps from a period of practice learning. If you have not had this opportunity, you could reflect on a practice case study, either from a book, or from your broader learning experience. Identify the different forms of knowledge and evidence that could support practice in that scenario. What examples of knowledge and evidence might be relevant and supportive of practice in that situation and why would they make a difference to practice? Examine your examples of knowledge; can you identify the source of each example?

Of course, we cannot predict your individual thoughts on this exercise, but would anticipate that you could identify a range of different forms of knowledge arising from different sources (skill 4). If you have the opportunity this is a particularly useful exercise when worked through with colleagues, either fellow students, practitioners, assessors or supervisors. Were you able to identify the sources of your knowledge examples? This is not always as straightforward as it may seem as sometimes there is an overlap. You could draw on Pawson et al.'s (2003) typology discussed above and in Chapters 2 and 3 to give you some categories to work to. You may also categorise your examples of knowledge into that which is scientific research-based knowledge and that which is less tangible knowledge. In doing so, you might consider whether one or other form would be more influential to the aspect of practice you are reflecting on (skill 7 and skill 8). Crucially, though, however you respond to this exercise, you should be able to articulate why you have selected those particular knowledge and evidence examples. To justify the value of that knowledge, you would need to have subjected it to critical examination (skill 3, skill 4 and skill 7). The importance of critical reflection and analysis when drawing on knowledge for social work practice has also been a theme throughout this book and, as such, is the focus of the next section of this chapter.

Critiquing the evidence and knowledge

Evidence and knowledge for social work practice needs to be subjected to critical reflection, scrutiny and interrogation to ensure it is relevant, reliable, trustworthy and contextually appropriate. Throughout this book we have encouraged you to think critically and to examine the validity of all forms of knowledge and the ways that knowledge is produced. As argued in Chapter 2, it is not always easy to establish that knowledge and evidence are 'right' or trustworthy. On the contrary, we live and practise in an uncertain world, where the view that knowledge is 'truth' is often difficult to sustain. As part of this evolution in our understanding of knowledge, universities are increasingly moving away from the traditional notion that lecturers are experts who hold a monopoly on knowledge and that students are 'empty vessels to be filled with facts' (Schwartz 2004: 27). Consequently there is recognition that study in higher education is but one activity in a student's life, and that all students bring with them a myriad of life experiences, knowledge and self-understanding to share (Burawoy 2005). Therefore every student's potential to contribute analytical, critical thinking (McLean 2008), knowledge and experience is recognised and built upon with universities highlighting the importance of creativity, criticality, investigation and questioning. This approach creates a more democratic learning environment which encourages students to actively contribute to the generation of knowledge, working with lecturers and tutors as 'co-producers' of knowledge.

Optional further study

For those of you who are interested in the subject of students being explicitly involved in the co-production of knowledge alongside other members of their academic community, **Healey and Jenkins** (2009) have produced a comprehensive guide to the development of 'undergraduate research and inquiry'. This accessible handbook talks about the rationale for such activity and the benefits that accrue from a more creative, democratic environment and provides examples of good practice drawn from across the world.

Similarly, as a social worker you need to be a critical, reflective thinker and this applies equally to your practice responsibilities and the evidence that you might read or use. The skills used in critical thinking help to develop precision in the way professionals think and work (Cottrell 2011). A social worker who is unable to extend their own learning, keep abreast of developments in the field and analyse initiatives and information will be increasingly dysfunctional. This is because change is a certainty as the social, demographic, legal and moral conditions in which people live and work do not stay constant.

The chapters in this book have supported your learning as reflective practitioner. In particular, in Chapter 3 you learnt about interrogating and questioning knowledge through reflective practice, taking a critical perspective on your own practice and your agency or organisation's culture and approaches (skill 3 and skill 7). Taking a critical approach requires proactive, creative thought; it is not a passive activity. Constructive critique requires you to deconstruct and consider the strengths and weaknesses in an argument, ensuring that your approach is non-judgemental and supported by evidence (skill 2 and skill 4). According to Brown and Rutter, 'thinking critically can result in major shifts in our ways of thinking and the development of reflective scepticism, i.e. when nothing is regarded as a universal truth or taken on trust' (2006: 2). As such, critical reflection may feel risky and difficult; indeed you may experience reflection in exactly this way, particularly when you question your own practice and the values, skills and knowledge that underpin it. However, in Chapters 3 and 6 and later in this chapter, we highlight the supportive, facilitative and developmental nature of processes such as supervision, provision for newly qualified social workers, and collegiate practices.

As a way of consolidating your understanding about ways to critique and analyse knowledge for practice, complete the following exercise.

Critical thinking exercise 7.2: Key elements of knowledge for practice

Reflect on your reading in this book about the notion of 'knowledge' and what it means for social work practice. What do you consider to be the key elements that you would now look for in 'knowledge' to inform your professional practice?

Responses to this exercise may vary greatly but, crucially, through your learning from the chapters in this book, we would anticipate that the key elements that you could look for when examining 'knowledge' to inform your practice would demonstrate your ability to question and scrutinise all evidence and knowledge (skill 4). Indeed you could frame your response into questions; we would suggest that there are potentially five key questions that you might use to interrogate knowledge for practice; you may have thought of others.

- How relevant is it to this practice context and need?
- Are the recommendations and outcomes clear, unambiguous and straightforward to apply to practice?
- How have the views and experiences of service users and carers influenced this knowledge?
- How has professional practice experience influenced this knowledge?
- In what ways does this knowledge contribute to and support effective professional practice, professional social work values and anti-oppressive practice?

You may also recall a similar exercise in Chapter 3 (Critical thinking exercise 3.3), following which you learnt about TAPUPA, the principles behind the assessment of social care knowledge (Pawson et al. 2003), so you may find it useful to review these principles now.

So far, in this final chapter, we have highlighted how different forms of evidence and knowledge are crucial aspects of the basis of social work, not only legitimising the profession but also informing moral and ethical reasoning, practice processes and decision-making.

Optional further study

At this point you may be interested to explore the issue of professional decision-making further. In particular you could look at the first chapter of

O'Sullivan, T. (2010) *Decision Making in Social Work* (2nd edition). Basingstoke: Palgrave Macmillan.

While you may focus on the first chapter, you will find this whole text of value, as O'Sullivan places decision-making as a core activity in social work, and considers issues of ethics, power, participation, interprofessional working and critical engagement with the knowledge base for practice.

Additionally we have taken this further through the second theme, to argue that all research and wider knowledge must be subjected to critical questioning and reflective approaches to practice. The following section of this chapter draws on elements of each of these first two themes, as the third key theme running through this book relates to the significance of service user and carer knowledge, and practice wisdom, for social work practice. Both of these latter sources of knowledge often sit outside of the scientific paradigm but should be subjected to the same levels of scrutiny.

The value of service user and carer knowledge to ethical professional practice

It is important to understand how knowledge that emanates from the views and perspectives of service users and carers provides an essential contribution to the research and knowledge that underpins and shapes ethical professional practice. Throughout this book we have used the phrase 'service user and carer knowledge' as a shorthand way to refer to that knowledge or evidence produced by service users, carers or others who have experience of receiving social care services. A key theme and argument through the chapters of this book is that this form of knowledge is integral to the sound, ethical implementation of social work practice. In this section of this concluding chapter, we will draw together the key learning points from across the book about service user and carer knowledge.

The discussion of service user knowledge commenced in Chapter 2 by exploring the important concept of power; in particular the disparity in power between the different groups of people involved in the production of evidence or knowledge. We drew on, for example, the work of Glasby and Beresford (2006) to exemplify the inherent power imbalance between service users and academics, and to demonstrate how service user knowledge is often debased or unvalued. This is reflective of a similar power divide between service users and social workers (Smith 2008). This, in turn, may mean that the difficulty academics have in interpreting and valuing the contribution of service users is mirrored by a similar lack of understanding by social workers in practice (skill 2). This recognition of power relations is vital to our overall analysis as, for example, it helps to explain the difference in the way that scientific and non-scientific evidence is perceived as discussed in the previous section of this chapter.

Optional further study

You may be interested to explore issues of power and empowerment in more depth than is possible here. The following sources offer a good starting point for such an exploration.

Smith, R. (2008) *Social Work and Power.* Basingstoke: Palgrave Macmillan.

Thompson, N. (2007) *Power and Empowerment.* Lyme Regis: Russell House.

Historically social work has used service user knowledge and experience 'to legitimise, rationalise and promote social work' (Beresford and Croft 2001: 300), a point that was discussed in Chapter 4 as we contextualised the debate about service user knowledge, the use of power and power dynamics. Additionally, these understandings have been used in related professional areas to assist in the construction of academic theory/ research and the development of managerial practice. These processes have often failed to acknowledge the extent or influence of service user knowledge, being explicitly based on the interpretation of that knowledge by the professional, as opposed to the user. In other words, those who organise, manage and deliver social work have often drawn on service user knowledge for their own purposes, rather than for the benefit of users. You may feel that this is a harsh overstatement for, quite rightly, all interpretations are open to question and challenge (skill 4). Nonetheless, it is important to acknowledge the influence of power and how this can be potentially used to promote or disqualify different perspectives (skill 3). Throughout the chapters of this book, however, we have sought to present a balanced approach, reflecting that some writers, for example Beresford and Croft (2001), feel that the contribution of service users is being increasingly acknowledged in the production of research, within education and training, and finally in the evaluation of service delivery.

Continuing our discussion of power, in Chapter 4 you learnt about two specific examples of service user knowledge, the development of the social model and the moves towards the personalisation of care; both examples involve a transition of power. The social model, which derives from the wider search for social justice in 1960s America, explicitly views the challenges faced by disabled people as having structural causation, as opposed to being a result of individual pathology or inability. We have argued that this radical view could be seen as a forerunner of anti-oppressive approaches in social work practice. Equally, the evolution of services (particularly adult services) towards a more personalised approach has been driven by the experiences of those who receive social care services. Both of these movements can be seen as examples of where service users have redefined the frameworks within which their lives are described and the knowledge which underpins the way in which services are delivered.

Further to this, within developments towards personalisation in social care, discussed in Chapter 4, the notion of 'co-production' is perceived as a particularly relevant philosophy (Hunter and Ritchie 2007: 11). Earlier in the chapter, you read about how learning in higher education is being increasingly characterised by a move away from expertise and certainty, with students being encouraged to participate in the creation of knowledge as 'co-producers'. You may identify more parallels between education and social work practice with an increasing emphasis on collaboration and partnership with other practitioners, other disciplines, carers and service users. With service user knowledge being recognised as that which is 'based on direct experience – on what people know from living through it – from being on the receiving end of policy and services' (Beresford 2005: 2).

Referring back again to the historical contextualisation offered in Chapter 4, a recurrent theme identified by Horner (2009) in his survey of the development of professional social work is that of the state, or the worker, 'doing things to' the individual in need. Traditionally, there is no sense of partnership or mutuality as the state identifies the problem, often cites it within the individual, sets the agenda and decides what the resolution is and what might be provided. Both the social model and contemporary moves towards the personalisation of care services radically shift the relationship and begin to grant a modicum of power and control to those who use services.

This possible drift of power away from the professional can also be detected in our discussion in Chapter 5, where we considered the role of service users and carers in the production of formal knowledge. In particular, we introduced you to the concepts of 'participatory' and 'emancipatory' research (Beresford and Croft 2001). Drawing on the work of Arnstein (1969) and the 'ladder of participation' (and Hart's 1992 development of it) we explored the redistribution of power in research. As Arnstein's (1969) and Hart's (1992) models describe relationships that are experienced at the higher rungs of the ladder as being more likely to be characterised by the user having increasing power in decision-making processes, so in research, service users are beginning to gain some control of research and the decisions that are made through the processes of research development.

While, arguably, formal research continues to be dominated by university-based 'white men in white coats', there is a momentum behind service user research which practitioners should value and encourage. It is important, however, to recognise that there is a need to be mindful of a number of limitations in working with service users in research (skill 4). To return again to Chapter 5, McLaughlin (2009) notes three major areas of difficulty.

- First, it is necessary to consider the amount of time that is required to train and prepare service users and carers to become competent researchers. This should not be underestimated as there is a considerable body of knowledge and skill that needs to be acquired before research can be undertaken.
- Second, the issue of ethics needs to be considered. Service users may personally know the subjects of the research or may have particular connections with a service or service provider. Consequently, research may be compromised or lack the necessary objectivity.
- Third, the issue of remuneration needs to be considered. However service users and carers are rewarded, it should be meaningful and reflect the level of expertise and engagement that they bring to the task.

Finally, an overall limitation we need to acknowledge when considering service user and carer knowledge is that, by definition, such research is subjective in nature and based on individual experience; this produces both advantages and disadvantages (skill 2). The advantages are that it derives from the real lived experience of people receiving services and provides a unique insight that practitioners, managers and academics need in order to inform their work. It also often produces far more practical outcomes than pure academic research as its motivation is to effect change in practice and services. The disadvantages are that it may be prone to bias and distortion, which can limit the validity of the knowledge and how it might be used to make recommendations that inform practice.

As a way of consolidating your learning about service user and carer knowledge and the knowledge that arises from practitioners, discussed as part of the first theme in this chapter, complete the following exercise.

Critical thinking exercise 7.3: Comparing and contrasting service user and carer knowledge with practitioner knowledge

Reflecting on your learning across this book, analyse some of the similarities and differences that you can identify between service user knowledge and practitioner knowledge.

Some areas of possible commonality that you may have considered are that both derive from *individual* experience and are subjective in nature. We need to recognise, however, that it is possible to generate *collective* types of this practice knowledge or practice wisdom through collegiate activity. The concept of 'communities of practice' is relevant here. Stemming from social learning theory, 'communities of practice' focus on identity (in this case professional identity), creativity and knowledge developed through social participation and interaction (Anning et al. 2010). In other words, working together, communicating and sharing practice ideas and dilemmas supports learning and generates knowledge, as in a team practitioners can '"achieve a cultural consensus and a shared discourse" which is not the result of "static agreement" . . . but is likely to be "a process"' (2010: 83). For example, a social work team may have gained considerable collective experience in working with a certain service user group or issue, sometimes over many years. Individual team members may come and go, but there remains a residue of 'team wisdom' that is passed down and refined by successive generations of workers. You read in Chapter 2, for example, aspects of practice which Pawson et al. (2003) suggest may lead to the acquisition and refinement of knowledge. These included team meetings, education, training, case conferences and sharing ideas. There are clearly dangers that this distilled wisdom may be out of date or inaccurate, so we need to be careful to provide a balanced view of intuitive knowledge as it can be 'unreliable, personal, [and] idiosyncratic' (O'Sullivan 2005: 222). Equally, this knowledge can be of immeasurable value as a means of providing the 'know-how' to address complex, evolving situations. This is particularly evident when considering the use and development of knowledge in interprofessional, multidisciplinary settings, which is explored in detail in Chapter 4.

Furthermore, in responding to this exercise you may have recognised the difference in that one type of knowledge is generated by the experience of receiving services and living with certain needs, while the other derives from the experience of assessing for and providing services (skill 2 and skill 4). Consequently, there are very different drivers or dynamics behind the production of knowledge. Practice wisdom may be influenced by organisational requirements, the practice of others or the life/professional experience of the practitioner. Service user knowledge, however, may be influenced by the personal situation of the user or carer, or past experiences of receiving services. There is also a difference in the way in which these types of knowledge are used. For the practitioner, practice wisdom assists them in understanding their role and in fulfilling their duties, while the service user is more interested in accessing, shaping and possibly using their acquired knowledge to inform other service users.

Chapter Summary

As the final summary of the last chapter in this book, it seems appropriate to revisit the reasons for embarking on this journey to understand evidence-based practice in social work. There are fundamental principles that underpin the rationale for social work practitioners and organisations needing to know about and using relevant knowledge, research and literature as a foundation for their day-to-day work. Some of the key principles are discussed below, in no particular order.

- Social work has a legal and policy basis which enables staff to make recommendations which enhance, or sometimes limit, the freedoms and daily lives of users. Those people who use services have a right to know that the judgements made, which affect them and their families, are made on something more robust than personal opinion. It is immoral to intervene in people's lives without any clear idea as to the potential effects of the work being undertaken and without knowing if their situation is likely to improve or be made worse as a result of the intervention. For example, it would be unethical to work with an older person towards the provision of permanent care in a residential setting and presenting it as a positive choice if you have not considered research into the effects of institutionalisation and balanced this with their views, their carer's views and the risk to that older person of remaining at home.
- Professional practice is dynamic, complex, multifaceted and often fluid; to help us deal with these intricacies we need to ensure that our practice is built on secure foundations. Research is a 'crucial component' of social work professionalism (D'Cruz and Jones 2004: 6); and a 'common sense approach' is not a valid professional concept. What any individual considers to be common sense is influenced by their upbringing, religion, education, social class, age, gender, culture, social norms and the policies and laws of the country in which an individual has grown up and the one in which they now live. Social workers are required to be critical thinkers and to apply knowledge to their practice. Doing whatever comes naturally may be damaging, especially if what comes naturally is prejudicial, ill-informed or plain wrong.
- Further to this, professional social work is characterised by critical reflective practice; this requires an underpinning knowledge base. Thinking about a situation and seeing the issues in a broader context can assist in reaching decisions about how to progress. As humans we are fortunate in having a brain and the capacity for thought and reflective learning. It can be stimulating to extend our knowledge and it is definitely rewarding if the increased knowledge has beneficial outcomes for service users and their carers. Most people expect professional workers to have a basis for their decisions and views and to evidence them if necessary. Indeed, the practice of social work is enhanced if a worker is able to demonstrate and articulate, for users and other colleagues, the rationale for action/inaction and some of the research and information that has guided their thinking. It is not viable to expect the public at large or other groups of professionals to have respect for social work as a profession, if it comes across as ill-informed and little more than instinctive. An ability to analyse evidence and to reflect on the validity of what has been researched, stated and read is an important social work skill.
- Social workers are increasingly required to argue their case in court settings, to formally established panels with executive powers, to inquiries and to committees of politicians and others with influence on service outcomes.

The people who sit on such panels and committees may have a varying understanding of social work practice and policy. They are usually interested in the specific evidence being presented to justify a course of action, especially when that action requires resources or the removal from home of a person against their will. Service users are better served by social workers who know what they are talking about and who can present a case with evidence, credibility and knowledge.

- Social work theory could not exist without the practice of social work, any more than social work could be sensibly practised without reference to research, knowledge and theory. Theorists and researchers use practice settings for research, exploring the outcomes for service users. The views of service users are increasingly considered in developing an understanding as to what it is like to be a recipient of social work practice. Additionally, service users and carers are becoming researchers and there are an increasing number of organisations that are promoting user- and practitioner-led research and making their findings accessible through articles, briefings, booklets and summary documents. Practitioners need to draw on the accumulated theoretical evidence to inform their understanding of the complex human and social issues to which they and their service users are exposed.
- Changes in social policy, strategic direction and practice guidance often emerge as a result of new information and evidence. You have seen how this happened with the example of the Victoria Climbié inquiry (Laming 2003) discussed earlier in this book. Social workers are required to both understand and implement policy; additionally they are often directly affected by it, as citizens and professionals, just as service users are. Change may be resisted by practitioners, particularly if the reasons for the changes are not understood and if the desired outcomes are not properly promoted. Hence there is a further reason for practitioners to be aware of the knowledge base that underpins strategy and policy direction. For example, over recent years the provision of care, support and educationally based services to very young children and their families has grown. This expansion of early years services results, at least in part, from evidence about the positive impact of pre-school learning on later educational attainment. Another example is the National Service Framework for Older People (Department of Health 2001), which was influenced by evidence gathered about the health and social care needs of older people, largely from older people themselves. Also, the Children (Care Leavers) Bill 2000 (DfE 2001) emerged from evidence that recorded the poor outcomes experienced by young people leaving care. These examples demonstrate that it is important for social workers to understand the evidence that results in policy change rather than simply finding change difficult, or feeling uneasy, if required to do something different.
- 'The effective pursuit of equality is seen as dependent on a properly informed analysis prior to the action' (D'Cruz and Jones 2004: 7). If, for instance, as a

social worker, you have not explored the research into the possible reasons for the overrepresentation of black people of African/African Caribbean origin in the mental health system you may perpetuate the very discrimination the profession is opposed to. If you simply absorb popular prejudice against asylum seekers with little knowledge of the circumstances of their lives and backgrounds, you could offer a service user an inappropriate or lesser service. If, working in childcare services, you have not understood some of the issues relating to the transracial placement of black children, you may continue discriminatory practices simply because this is how it has always been done. If sexist attitudes, discriminatory and subtle behaviours are unchallenged, certain actions that are detrimental to either males or females may be accepted as 'normal'. It could therefore be argued that a social worker who understands little beyond the technical requirements of the role is ineffective and negates the values and ethics necessary for the work.

In addition this chapter, and indeed this book, has encouraged you to actively engage with and develop a range of critical thinking skills. The chapter has been structured around three core themes that are threaded throughout this book; the concluding comments to each of these three sections identify the particular critical thinking skills that will be developed through your study of that theme.

As we warned in the introduction to this book, given the breadth and fluidity of the subject area it is unlikely that we will provide many cast-iron answers. But we hope that you have found the debate stimulating and are encouraged to further explore the knowledge that underpins professional practice.

Further reading

Brown, K. and Rutter, L. (2006) *Critical Thinking for Social Work.* (2nd edition) Exeter: Learning Matters.

Part of the Learning Matters post-qualifying social work practice series, this text includes a specific chapter (3) on 'applying new knowledge to practice'. Additionally, there are chapters that explore critical practice, critical thinking and critical reflection. Some of the key themes we have set out in this book reinforce the work of Brown and Rutter, in particular the importance of 'a critical overall disposition or stance' to the enhancement of effective professional practice (2008: 44).

Cottrell, S. (2011) *Critical Thinking Skills: Developing Effective Analysis and Argument* (2nd edition). Basingstoke: Palgrave Macmillan.

This book sets out to support the development of reflective thinking skills and critical analysis; it is written in a clear way, with examples, explanations and exercises. This is a generic study skills book, so while not specifically about social work, it can help you to develop your understanding and ability to draw on these skills, which are crucial for practice.

Shaping our Lives www.shapingourlives.org.uk
On the home page of their website, the national user network Shaping Our Lives explains that it is an independent user-controlled organisation that started as a research and development project and became an independent organisation in 2002. Shaping Our Lives seeks funding from different bodies for different projects to support the development of local user involvement that aims to deliver better outcomes for service users. There are a number of publications including research papers freely downloadable from their website.

Glossary

Anti-oppressive practice	Social Work practice that recognises oppressive social forces in society and seeks to promote social justice	Referred to throughout the book
Evidence	Information generated by scientific research. Often viewed as being a superior form of knowledge	Defined in Chapter 1 and referred to throughout the book
Evidence-based practice	Professional practice which is guided, support and informed by evidence	Defined in Chapter 1 and referred to throughout the book
General Social Care Council (GSCC)	The professional body responsible for the registration of social care staff	Mentioned throughout the book
Globalisation	Social trends characterised by the mass movement of workers across national boundaries, the use of power by multinational organisations, and the influence of information technologies which span the globe	A concept explored in Chapter 6 to highlight that knowledge is often culturally and geographically specific
Ideal type	An ideal type is a sociological concept devised by Max Weber. It is an idealised description which draws on the key characteristics and attributes of the phenomenon being studied, but does not necessarily describe reality	Used in Chapters 1 and 2 to describe some of our key terms such as 'knowledge' and 'evidence'
Interprofessional practice	Practice which is jointly undertaken using the skills, insights and knowledge of a range of professionals often drawn from a variety of organisations	A key aspect of Chapter 4
Knowledge	Theories, explanations, understandings and experiences which combine to tentatively inform and guide professional practice	Defined in Chapter 1 and referred to throughout the book
Knowledge classification or categorisation	Ways of grouping the different components of knowledge together to make them more understandable	Explained in Chapter 1 through the provision of several examples

Newly Qualified Social Worker framework (NQSW)	A package of measures introduced by the government in recent years to assist newly qualified staff make the adjustment between qualifying studies and full-time practice. Includes workload relief, mentorship, supervision and further training	Discussed in Chapter 6 and used as an example of changes within the profession which have impacted on knowledge
Organisational knowledge	Knowledge generated by managers, policymakers and practitioners within organisations, through the management, oversight and governance of social care	Defined in Chapter 1 and referred to throughout the book. A key component in the Pawson et al. (2003) typology of knowledge
Personalisation	The underpinning philosophy of Personalisation views the service user as someone with strengths, preferences and aspirations. This stands in contrast to traditional methods of service delivery where the person often had to fit in with organisational schedules, limitations and barriers outside of their control. The person is central to the process and is given as much choice and control over their care plan as possible	Personalisation was identified in Chapter 4 as being an example of service user knowledge which has informed and guided social work practice
Policy community knowledge	Knowledge which arises from the wider strategic and policy environment. This would include institutional reviews, audits, commissions and 'think tank' outputs	Defined in Chapter 1 and referred to throughout the book. A key component in the Pawson et al. (2003) typology of knowledge
Post-registration training and learning	Further training and learning undertaken by social workers following qualification. Often linked to the PQ (Post- qualifying) framework	Discussed in Chapter 5 and identified as one reason why practitioners may choose to engage in research
Practitioner knowledge	Knowledge generated from the experience, practice wisdom, tacit knowledge and reflective practice of those engaged in social care practice. This would include direct practitioner research	Defined in Chapter 1 and referred to throughout the book. A key component in the Pawson et al. (2003) typology of knowledge
(The) Professional Capabilities Framework for Social Workers in England	A key recommendation of the Social Work Task Force was the creation of a framework which established clear expectations of what social workers should know and be able to do at each stage of their career. While the framework is currently only a proposal it is highly likely to be implemented	Discussed in Chapter 6 and used as an example of changes within the profession which have impacted on knowledge

(The) Quality Assurance Agency Subject Benchmarks for Social Work	Subject benchmark statements describe what gives a discipline its coherence and identity, and define what can be expected of a graduate in terms of the abilities and skills needed to develop understanding or competence in the subject	Used at the beginning of each chapter to guide study and to make links with areas of professional development
Recovery model of mental health	The recovery model places an emphasis on the service user's lived experience and states that recovery from mental illness is possible in 'whatever form this takes for the individual' (**Bogg** 2008: 47). While it relies heavily on psychosocial understandings, it does not dismiss the efficacy of medical intervention as long as this actively contributes to the recovery of the person	Used in Chapter 4 to exemplify how interprofessional working has led to the creation of new shared knowledge
Research knowledge	Knowledge which is gathered systematically with predetermined design, including empirical inquiries, evaluations and evaluative reports	Defined in Chapter 1 and referred to throughout the book. A key component in the Pawson et al. (2003) typology of knowledge
Reflection	The act of critically considering practice. This can be an internal thought process or can be done with other people	Defined in Chapter 3. We argued that this was one of the principle ways in which a practitioner could interrogate knowledge
SCIE (The Social Care Institute for Excellence)	The social care body responsible for the product ion and dissemination of research, knowledge and good practice to practitioners	Mentioned throughout the book
Social model	The social model (of disability) can be seen as a derivative of the Civil Rights movement in 1960s America. It was argued that it was not so much physical impairment which disabled people but the way in which society systematically isolated and excluded people with disabilities	The social model was identified in Chapter 4 as being an example of service user knowledge which has informed and guided social work practice
Social Work Reform Board	In 2008 the Government established the *Social Work Task Force* to conduct a review of the profession and to advise on a comprehensive reform programme for social work. The Task Force produced its final report (HM Government 2009) in December 2009. This provided a set of 15 far-reaching recommendations; these are being taken forward by the *Social Work Reform Board*	Discussed in Chapter 6 and used as an example of changes within the profession which have impacted on knowledge

Spirituality	A recognition that the human spirit exists and has importance to the well-being of the person	Discussed in Chapter 6 and used as an example of an aspect of knowledge which social workers may be uncomfortable exploring
Students as researchers	Increasingly students are being used to assist with, or even lead, academic research. Sometimes linked to the idea of 'students as producers' which has a wider remit looking at how students can generate knowledge using a variety of methods	Discussed in Chapter 5 and used as an example of how different stakeholders are increasingly used to produce knowledge
Supervision	Supervision can occur in a number of different ways but is traditionally configured, at least in statutory social work, as a forum where a worker and supervisor (typically the line manager) meet together to discuss an amalgam of casework, organisational and managerial issues	Defined in Chapter 3. We argued that this was one of the principle ways in which a practitioner could interrogate knowledge
TAPUPA	An acronym devised by Pawson et al. (2003) to describe a number of ways in which knowledge could be evaluated	Principally explained in Chapter 3. The acronym stands for Transparency; Accuracy; Purposivity; Utility; Propriety; Accessibility
User and Carer knowledge	Knowledge which arises directly from the experience and reflections of service users and carers	Defined in Chapter 1 and referred to throughout the book. A key component in the Pawson et al. (2003) typology of knowledge
User-controlled research	Research which is planned, led, conducted and disseminated by service users. Often this type of research has a transformatory emphasis which concentrates on changing service provision	Discussed in Chapter 5
Values	The underpinning, non-negotiable ethics and morals which guide personal and professional behaviour. Social work is informed by a number of value requirements deriving from such organisations as the GSCC	Referred to throughout the book. In particular, interconnections are actively highlighted between values, knowledge and practice

References

Adams, R. Dominelli, L. and Payne,M. (eds) (2009a) *Social Work: Themes, Issues and Critical Debates* (3rd edition). Basingstoke: Palgrave Macmillan.

Adams, R. Dominelli, L. and Payne, M. (eds) (2009b) *Practising Social Work in a Complex World* (2nd edition). Basingstoke: Palgrave Macmillan.

Anning, A. Cottrell, D., Frost, N., Green, J. and Robinson, M. (2010) *Developing Multiprofessional Teamwork for Integrated Children's Services: Research, Policy and Practice* (2nd edition). Berkshire: Open University Press.

Arnstein, S. R. (1969) A Ladder of Citizen Participation. *Journal of the American Institute of Planners,* 35 (4): 216–24.

Baskin, C. (2002) Circles of Resistance: Spirituality in Social Work Practice, Education and Transformative Change. *Currents: New Scholarship in Human Services,* 1 (1): 1–9. Available at **www.ucalgary.ca/currents/files/currents/v1n1_baskin.pdf**

Becker, S. and Bryman, A. (2004) *Understanding Research for Social Policy and Practice: Themes, Methods and Approaches.* Bristol: The Policy Press.

Beresford, P. (2000) Service Users' Knowledge and Social Work Theory: Conflict or Collaboration *British Journal of Social Work,* 30 (4): 489–503.

Beresford, P. (2005) *Developing Knowledge-Based Practice — Context and Background.* Presentation to a symposium, 15 July 2005, British Society of Gerontology Annual Conference, Keele University. Available at **www2.warwick.ac.uk/fac/soc/shss/mrc/olderpeople/bsg/beresford.pdf**

Beresford, P. (2008) *What Future for Care?* York: The Joseph Rowntree Foundation.

Beresford, P. and Croft, S. (2001), Service Users, Knowledges and the Social Construction Of Social Work. *Journal of Social Work,* 1 (3): 295–316.

Blom, B. (2009) Knowing or Un-knowing? That is the Question: In the Era of Evidence Based Social Work Practice. *Journal of Social Work,* 9 (2): 158–77.

Bogg, D. (2008) *The Integration of Mental Health Social Work and the NHS.* Exeter: Learning Matters.

Bogg, D. (2010) *Values and Ethics in Mental Health Practice.* Exeter: Learning Matters.

Brandon, M., Dodsworth, J. and Rumball, R. (2005) Serious Case Reviews: Learning to Use Expertise. *Child Abuse Review,* 14: 160–76.

Brandon, M., Bailey, S. and Belderson, P. (2010) *Building on the Learning from Serious Case Reviews: A Two Year Analysis of Child Protection Database Notifications 2007–2009: Research Brief.* London: Department for Education.

Branfield, F. and Beresford, P. (2006) *Making User Involvement Work: Supporting Service User Networking and Knowledge.* York: The Joseph Rowntree Foundation.

Brookfield, S. (2009) The Concept of Critical Reflection: Promises and Contradictions. *European Journal of Social Work,* 12 (3): 293–304.

Brown, K. and Rutter, L. (2006) *Critical Thinking for Social Work.* Exeter: Learning Matters.

Buck, J. (2007) Social Work Placements; A Student Perspective. *Journal of Practice Teaching and Learning,* 7 (1): 6–12.

Burawoy, M. (2005) American Sociological Association Presidential Address: For Public Sociology, *American Sociological Review*. 70 (1): 4–28.

Carr, S. (2010) *Personalisation: A Rough Guide*. Adults' Services Reports 20. London: SCIE.

Children's Workforce Development Council (2010) *NQSW Outcome statements and guidance*. Newly Qualified Social Worker Programme. Leeds: CWDC.

Cochrane, S. (ed.) (2004) *Where you Stand Affects your Point of View. Emancipatory Approaches to Mental Health Research*. SPN study day, June 2003.

Coleman, R. (1999) *Recovery an Alien Concept?* Gloucester: Handsell.

Corby, B. (2006) *Applying Research in Social Work Practice*. Maidenhead: Open University Press.

Cottrell, S. (2011) *Critical Thinking Skills: Developing Effective Analysis and Argument*. Basingstoke: Palgrave Macmillan.

Cunningham J. and Cunningham S. (2009) *Sociology and Social Work*. Exeter: Learning Matters.

D'Cruz, H. and Jones, M. (2004) *Social Work Research: Ethical and Political Contexts*. London: Sage.

Department for Children, Schools and Families (DCSF) (2004) *The Children Act*. London: HMSO.

Department for Education (2001) *The Children (Care Leavers) Bill 2000*. London: HMSO.

Department of Health (DOH) (1995) *Child Protection; Messages from Research*. London: HMSO.

Department of Health (2001) *The National Service Framework for Older People*. London: HMSO.

Dewey, J. (1910) *How we Think*. Boston MA: DC Heath.

Dickens, S. and Woodfield, K. (2004) *New Approaches to Youth Homelessness: A Qualitative Evaluation of the Safe in the City Cluster Scheme*. York: The Joseph Rowntree Foundation.

Dreyfus, H.L. and Dreyfus, S.E. (1986) *Mind over Machine: The Power of Human Intuition and Expertise in the Era of the Computer*. Oxford: Basil Blackwell.

Durkheim, E. (2002) *Suicide; A Study in Sociology*. London: Routledge.

Epstein, R.M. (1999) Mindful Practice. *Journal of the American Medical Association*, 282 (9): 833–9.

Eraut, M. (1995) Schön Shock: A Case for Reframing Reflection in Action. *Teachers and Teaching*, 1 (1): 9–22.

Fallon, P., Bluglass, R., Edwards, B. and Daniels, G. (1999) *Report of the Committee of Inquiry into the Personality Disorder Unit, Ashworth Special Hospital*. London: Department of Health.

Ferguson, I. and Woodward, R. (2009) *Radical Social Work in Practice: Making a Difference*. Bristol: Policy Press.

Foucault, M. (1980) *Power/Knowledge: Selected Interviews and Other Writings 1972–77* (ed) Gordon, C. New York: Pantheon Books.

Fuller, R. and Petch, A. (1995) *Practitioner Research. The Reflexive Social Worker*. Buckingham: Open University Press.

Gaine, C. (ed.) (2010) *Equality and Diversity in Social Work Practice*. Exeter: Learning Matters.

General Medical Council (2010) Fitness to Practise Panel Hearing, 28 January. Available at **www.gmc-uk.org**

Gibbons, M., Limoges, C., Nowotny, H., Schwartzman, S., Scott, P. and Trow, M. (1994) *The New Production of Knowledge: Dynamics of Science and Research in Contemporary Societies*. London: Sage.

Gilgun, J.F. (2005) The Four Cornerstones of Evidence Based Practice in Social Work. *Research on social work practice*, 15 (1): 52–61.

Giroux, H. (1988) *Teachers as Intellectuals: Towards a Critical Pedagogy of Learning*. Westport: Bergin and Garvey.

Glasby, J. (2005) Paper One: The Future of Adult Social Care: Lessons from Previous Reforms. *Research Policy and Planning*, 23 (2): 61–70.

Glasby, J. and Beresford, P. (2006) Who Knows Best? Evidence Based Practice and the Service User Contribution. *Critical Social Policy*, 26: 268–83.

Glynn, T. (2004) There is a Better Way. Chapter 12 in Cochrane, S. (ed.) *Where you Stand Affects your Point of View. Emancipatory Approaches to Mental Health Research.* SPN study day, June 2003.

Golightley, M. (2009) *Social Work and Mental Health* (3rd edition). Exeter: Learning Matters.

Gould, N. (2010) *Mental Health Social Work in context.* Abingdon: Routledge.

Hamer, S. and Collinson, G. (1999) *Achieving Evidence-Based Practice.* Edinburgh: Bailliere Tindall.

Hardwick, L. and Worsley, A. (2011) *Doing Social Work Research.* London: Sage.

Haringey Local Safeguarding Children Board (2009) *Serious Case Review: Baby Peter Executive Summary.* Available at **www.haringeylscb.org.uk**

Harris, J. (2003) *The Social Work Business.* Routledge: London.

Hart, R. (1992) *Children's Participation: From Tokenism to Citizenship.* Innocenti Essay No. 4. Florence, Italy: UNICEF International Child Development Center. Available at www.unicef-irc.org/publications/pdf/childrens_participation.pdf

Healey, M. (2005) Linking Teaching and Research Exploring Disciplinary Spaces and the Role of Inquiry based learning. In Barnett, R. (ed.) *Reshaping the University: New Relationships between Research, Scholarship and Teaching.* Maidenhead: McGraw-Hill/Open University Press.

Healey, M. and Jenkins, A. (2009) *Developing Undergraduate Research and Inquiry.* York: The Higher Education Academy.

HM Government (2007) *Putting People First: A Shared Vision and Commitment to the Transformation of Adult Social Care.* London: HM Government.

HM Government (2009) *Building a Safe and Confident Future: The Final Report of the Social Work Taskforce.* London: Department for Children, Schools and Families.

HM Government (2010) *Building a Safe and Confident Future: One year on. Detailed Proposals from the Social Work Reform Board.* London: Department for Children, Schools and Families.

HMSO (2003) *Every Child Matters.* Norwich: HMSO.

Horner, N. (2009) *What is Social Work? Context and Perspectives* (3rd edition). Exeter: Learning Matters.

Hunter, S. and Ritchie, P. (2007) Introduction — With, Not To: Models of Co-Production in Social Welfare. In Hunter, S. and Ritchie, P. (eds) *Co-Production and Personalisation in Social Care: Changing Relationships in the Provision of Social Care.* London: Jessica Kingsley.

International Federation of Social Workers (2000) Definition of Social Work. Available at **www.ifsw.org**

Ixer, G. (1999) There's no such Thing as Reflection. *British Journal of Social Work,* 29 (6): 513–27.

Johnstone, L. (2009) Twenty five years of disagreeing with psychiatry. Chapter 5 in Reynolds, J., Muston, R., Heller, T., Leach, J., McCormick, M., Wallcraft, J. and Walsh, M. (eds) *Mental Health Still Matters.* Basingstoke: Palgrave Macmillan.

Jones, S. (2009) *Critical Learning for Social Work Students.* Exeter: Learning Matters.

Keen, S., Gray, I., Parker, J., Galpin, D. and Brown, K. (eds) (2009) *Newly Qualified Social Workers: A Handbook for Practice.* Exeter: Learning Matters.

Laming, H. (2003) *The Victoria Climbié Inquiry Report,* Cm 5730. London: The Stationery Office. Available at: **www.victoria-climbie-inquiry.org.uk**.

Laming, H (2009). *The Protection of Children in England: A Progress Report.* London: The Stationery Office.

Lawrence-Jones, J. (2010) Dual Diagnosis (Drug/Alcohol and Mental Health). Service User Experiences. *Practice: Social Work in Action,* 22 (2): 115–31.

Lomax, R., Jones, K., Leigh, S. and Gay, C. (2010) *Surviving your Social Work Placement.* Basingstoke: Palgrave Macmillan.

Lymbery, M. and Millward, A. (2009) Partnership Working. Chapter 13 in Adams, R., Dominelli, L. and Payne, M. (eds) *Practising Social Work in a Complex World* (2nd edition). Basingstoke: Palgrave MacMillan.

Manthorpe, J. and Stanley, N. (eds) (2004) *The Age of the Inquiry. Learning and Blaming in Health and Social Care.* Basingstoke: Routledge.

Mathews, I (2009) *Social Work and Spirituality.* Exeter: Learning Matters.

McKimm, J. and Phillips, K. (eds) (2009) *Leadership and Management in Integrated Services.* Exeter: Learning Matters.

McLaughlin, H. (2007) *Understanding Social Work Research.* London: Sage.

McLaughlin, H. (2009) Researching Social Work. Chapter 12 in Adams, R., Dominelli, L. and Payne, M. (eds) *Social work; Themes, Issues and Critical Debates* (3rd edition). Basingstoke: Palgrave Macmillan.

McLean, M. (2008) *Pedagogy and the University.* London: Continuum.

Mitchell, F., Lunt, N. and Shaw, I. (2008) *Practitioner Research in Social Services: A Literature Review.* IRISS. York: University of York.

Morrison, T. (2005) *Staff Supervision in Social Care: Making a Real Difference for Staff and Service Users.* Brighton: Pavilion Publishing Ltd.

Moss, B. (2005) *Religion and Spirituality.* Lyme Regis: Russell House.

Mulally, R. (1993) *Structural Social Work: Ideology, Theory and Practice.* Toronto: McClelland and Stewart.

Murray, C. (1990) *The Emerging British Underclass.* London: Institute of Economic Affairs Health and Welfare Unit.

Nathan, J. (2002) The Advanced Practioner: Beyond Reflection Practice. *Journal of Practice Teaching,* 4 (2): 59–83.

Noble, C. (1999) The Elusive Yet Essential Project of Developing Field Education as a Legitimate Area of Social Work Inquiry. *Issues in Social Work Education,* 19 (1): 2–16.

Noble, C. and Irwin, J. (2009) Social Work Supervision: An Exploration of the Current Challenges in a Rapidly Changing Social, Economic and Political Environment. *Journal of Social Work,* (9): 345–58.

Nygren, L. and Soydan, H. (1997) Social Work Research and its Dependence on Practice. *Scandinavian Journal of Social Welfare,* 6: 217–24.

O'Hagan, K. (1994) Crisis Intervention: Changing Perspectives. In Harvey, C. and Philpot, T. (eds) *Practising Social Work.* London: Routledge.

Oliver, M. (1996) *Understanding Disability: From Theory to Practice.* Basingstoke: Macmillan.

Osmond, J., Scott, T. and Clark, J. (2008) The Knowledge of Caring: Revisiting the Need for Knowledge Support of Carers. *Child and Family Social Work,* 13: 262–73.

O'Sullivan, T. (2005) Some Theoretical Propositions on the Nature of Practice Wisdom. *Journal of Social Work* 5 (2): 221–42.

O'Sullivan, T. (2010) *Decision Making in Social Work* (2nd edition). Basingstoke: Palgrave Macmillan.

Parker, J. (2004) *Effective Practice Learning in Social Work.* Exeter: Learning Matters.

Parton, N. (2004) From Maria Colwell to Victoria Climbié; Reflections on Public Inquiries into Child Abuse a Generation Apart. *Child Abuse Review,* 13: 80–94.

Parton, N. (2008) Changes in the Form of Knowledge in Social Work: From the 'Social' to the 'Informational'. *British Journal of Social Work,* 38: 253–69.

Pawson, R., Boaz, A., Grayson, L., Long, A. and Barnes, C. (2003) *Types and Quality of Knowledge in Social Care. Knowledge review 3.* London: SCIE.

Payne, M. (1996) *What is Professional Social Work?* Birmingham: Venture.

Payne, M. (2001) Knowledge Bases and Knowledge Biases in Social Work. *Journal of Social Work*, (1): 133–46.

Payne, M. (2009) Doing Literature Searches and Reviews. Chapter 21 in Adams, R., Dominelli, L. and Payne, M. (eds) *Practising Social Work in a Complex World* (2nd edition). Basingstoke: Palgrave Macmillan.

Payne, M. and Askeland, G.A. (2008) *Globalization and International Social Work: Postmodern Change and Challenge*. London: Ashgate.

Pitcher, D. and Arnill, M (2010) Allowed to be There: The Wider Family and Child Protection. *Practice: Social Work in Action*, 22 (1): 17–31.

Quality Assurance Agency for Higher Education (2008) *Subject Benchmarks for Social Policy and Administration and Social Work*. Gloucester: QAA.

Rabiee, P., Moran, N. and Glendinning, C. (2009) Individual Budgets: Lessons from Early Users' Experiences. *British Journal of Social Work*, 39 (5): 918–35.

Reynolds, J., Muston, R., Heller, T., Leach, J., McCormick, M., Wallcraft, J. and Walsh, M. (eds) (2009) *Mental Health Still Matters*. Basingstoke: Palgrave Macmillan.

Richardson, G., Chiswick, D. and Nutting, I. (1997) *Report of the Inquiry into the Treatment and Care of Darren Carr*. Reading: Berkshire Health Authority.

Roberts, R. (2000) *Crisis Intervention Handbook: Assessment, Treatment and Research* (2nd edition). Oxford: Oxford University Press.

Rolfe, G., Freshwater, D. and Jasper, M. (2001) *Critical Reflection for Nursing and the Helping Professions: A User's Guide*. London: Palgrave Macmillan.

Schön, D. (1983) *The Reflective Ppractitioner*. London: Temple Smith.

Schwartz, S. (2004) Time to Bid Goodbye to the Psychology Lecture. *The Psychologist*, 17 (1): 26–7.

SCIE (2004a) *ADHD — Background, Assessment and Diagnosis*. Research briefing 7. Available at **www.scie.org.uk**

SCIE (2004b) *Improving the Use of Research in Social Care Practice*. London: Social Care Institute for Excellence.

SCIE (2005) *Developing the Evidence Base for Social Work and Social Care Practice*. Social Care Report 10. London: Social Care Institute for Excellence.

Scull, A.T. (1993) *The Most Solitary of Afflictions: Madness and Society in Britain, 1700–1900*. New Haven: Yale University Press.

Seebohm, F. (1968) *Report of the Committee on Local Authority and Allied Personal Social Services*. London: HMSO.

Sheldon, B. and Chilvers, R. (2002) *Evidence-Based Social Care: A Study of Prospects and Problems*. Lyme Regis: Russell House.

Sheppard, M., Newstead, S., DiCaccavo, A. and Ryan, K. (2000) Reflexivity and the Development of Process Knowledge in Social Work: A Classification and Empirical Study. *British Journal of Social Work*, 30: 465–88.

Simpkin, M. (1983) *Trapped within Welfare* (2nd edition). London: Macmillan.

Simpson, D., Mathews, I., Croft, A., McKinna, G. and Lee, M. (2010) Student views on good practice in social work education. *Social Work Education: The International Journal*, 29 (7): 729–43.

Singh, G. and Cowden, S. (2009) The Social Worker as Intellectual. *European Journal of Social Work*, 12 (4): 479–93.

Smith, C. (2001) Trust and Confidence: Possibilities for Social Work in High Modernity. *British Journal of Social Work*, 32 (2): 287–306.

Smith, C. (2004) Trust and Confidence: Making the Moral Case for Social Work in High Modernity. *Social Work and Social Services Review*, 11 (3): 5–15.

Smith, R. (2008) Social Work and Power. Basingstoke: Palgrave Macmillan.

Solway, R.A. (1995) *Demography and Degeneration. Eugenics and the Declining Birth Rate in Twentieth Century Britain.* London: The University of North Carolina Press.

Stalker, K. (2003) Managing Risk and Uncertainty in Social Work. *Journal of Social Work,* 3 (2): 211–33.

Stanley, N. and Manthorpe, J. (2001) Reading Mental Health Inquiries: Messages for Social Work. *Journal of Social Work,* 1 (1): 77–99.

Tate, S. and Sills, M. (eds) (2004) *The Development of Critical Reflection in The Health Professions.* Occasional Paper 4. London: LTSN (Health Science and Practice).

Taylor, B. (2010) *Professional Decision Making in Social Work Practice.* Exeter: Learning Matters.

Taylor, C. and White, S. (2000) *Practising Reflexivity in Health and Welfare.* Buckingham: Open University Press.

Thompson, N. (2006) *Anti-Discriminatory Practice* (4th edition). Basingstoke: Palgrave Macmillan.

Thompson, N. (2007) *Power and Empowerment.* Lyme Regis: Russell House.

Thompson, S. and Thompson, N. (2008) *The Critically Reflective Practitioner.* Basingstoke: Palgrave MacMillan.

TOPSS (2002) *The National Occupational Standards for Social Work.* Leeds: TOPSS.

Trevithick, P. (2005) *Social Work Skills: A Practice Handbook* (2nd edition). Milton Keynes: Open University Press.

Trevithick, P. (2007) Revisiting the Knowledge Base of Social Work: A Framework for Practice. *British Journal of Social Work,* 38: 1212–37.

Trivedi, P. (2009) Are We Who We Say We Are or Who You Think We Are?, Chapter 34 in Reynolds, J., Muston, R., Heller, T., Leach, J., McCormick, M., Wallcraft, J. and Walsh, M. (eds) *Mental Health Still Matters.* Basingstoke: Palgrave MacMillan.

Trinder, L. (2000) A Critical Appraisal of Evidence-Based Practice. In Trinder, L. and Reynolds, S. (eds) *Evidence-based Practice: A Critical Appraisal.* Oxford: Blackwell Science.

Turner, M. and Beresford, P. (2005) *User Controlled Research: Its Meanings and Potential.* Final Report Shaping Our Lives and the Centre for Citizen Participation, Brunel University. Eastleigh: Involve.

Twigg, J. and Atkin, K. (1994) *Carers Perceived: Policy and Practice in Informal Care.* Buckingham: Open University Press.

Walker, H. (2008) *Studying for your Social Work Degree.* Exeter: Learning Matters.

Ward, M. and Applin, C. (1998) *The Unlearned Lesson. The Role of Alcohol and Drug Misuse in Homicides Perpetrated by People with Mental Health Problems. A Study of Seventeen Reports of Inquiries into Homicides by Mentally Ill People.* London: Wynne Howard Publishing.

Warren, J. (2007) *Service User and Carer Participation in Social Work.* Exeter: Learning Matters.

Wells, A. (2009) My Right to Choose. Chapter 37 in Reynolds, J., Muston, R., Heller, T., Leach, J., McCormick, M., Wallcraft, J. and Walsh, M. (eds) *Mental Health Still Matters.* Basingstoke: Palgrave Macmillan.

Westbrook, R. B. (1993) John Dewey. *Prospects,* XXIII (1\2): 277–91.

Wilson, K., Ruch, G., Lymbery, M. and Cooper, A. (2008) *Social Work. An Introduction to Contemporary Practice.* Harlow: Pearson Education Limited.

Wood, J., Ashman, M., Davies, C., Lloyd, H. and Lockett, K. (1996) *Report of the Inquiry into the Care of Anthony Smith.* Derby: Southern Derbyshire Health Authority/Derbyshire County Council.

Younghusband, E. (1947) *Report on the Education and Training of Social Workers.* Edinburgh: Edinburgh University Press.

Index

Added to a page number 'f' denotes a figure, 't' denotes a table and 'g' denotes glossary.